M000195584

STREETSMART PROJECT MANAGEMENT

STREETSMART PROJECT MANAGEMENT

THE ART OF GETTING THINGS DONE

ERIK LANGE

Copyright © 2021 by Erik A. Lange
Written and published by Erik Lange

All rights reserved.

This book or any portion thereof may not be reproduced or used in any manner whatsoever without the express written permission of the publisher except for the use of brief quotations in a book review.

The publisher and the author make no guarantees concerning the level of success you may experience by following the advice and strategies contained in this book, and you accept the risk that results will differ for each individual.

Unless otherwise indicated, all the names, characters, businesses, places, events and incidents in this book are either the product of the author's imagination or used in a fictitious manner. Any resemblance to actual persons, living or dead, or actual events is purely coincidental.

Although the publisher and the author have made every effort to ensure that the information in this book was correct at press time and while this publication is designed to provide accurate information in regard to the subject matter covered, the publisher and the author assume no responsibility for errors, inaccuracies, omissions, or any other inconsistencies herein and hereby disclaim any liability to any party for any loss, damage, or disruption caused by errors or omissions, whether such errors or omissions result from negligence, accident, or any other cause.

Cover art by Shane Almgren

First Printing, 2021

First edition (paperback)

ISBN 978-1-7324326-6-6

This book is dedicated to the beta readers extraordinaire:
Andy Gagnon, Charlotte Smith, Doug Fry, Dr. Owe Petersen,
and Paul Rowlett .

Introduction

I spent a month of training at a corporate headquarters in Germany. The instructor was a German with a doctorate in physics, from a German university, and who worked in the industry for more than 30 years. Brilliant man. It was a truly unique learning opportunity.

Toward the end of the training, I asked about a technical detail. The instructor said he did not have the answer; there are things about the subject that are still not understood.

Wait? What? There are things nobody has the answers to? But he was an educated, experienced subject-matter expert. How could he not know? Honestly, I was almost speechless.

What do you mean, nobody knows what is going on?

This experience reinforced my understanding that there is still a lot of mystery in the world. There are observed phenomena no one has figured out yet. There are unknown's smart people have been studying for literally centuries that remain unsolved.

This realization, that there are things no one can explain, is the first step in a journey to realizing this also applies to the human equation. There are unknowns as to why people do what they do. Unfortunately, these poorly understood human behaviors have real-world implications. And project management is a very human endeavor.

This book addresses the in-between space in project management. The repeating people, communication, and process interactions that make up the phenomena observed in the project management environment. Through inspection of these phenomena, you will gain the awareness and develop the expertise to constructively engage these challenges and opportunities.

There are times in your professional life when you will wonder what is going on. Why is this so difficult? Should this be like this? Did I miss a training opportunity and now I do not know what everyone else knows? Am I smart enough to be doing this? A disturbing aspect of witnessing these unknowns is watching colleagues you respect performing a collaborative task and the results make you question if they know what they are doing.

Observing something and not understanding why it is happening is stressful. You realize that what you are involved in does not make sense. Or at least you do not understand it.

Witnessing these phenomena is perhaps what it might be like to see a ghost. You watch project management dynamics play out over and over again. Then you look at your colleagues to see if they are seeing what you are seeing. Is it supposed to be like this? What am I missing?

This exact experience drove my search for solutions and the creation of this book. To find a way to influence events toward success—or to just understand so I could cope.

Having someone tap you on the shoulder and validate your observation makes a difference. It's confirmation you are not seeing ghosts. That it is real. It happened, and there is an opportunity for improvement.

This book is a collection of observed phenomena and the tools useful in driving projects to completion. It is intended as a reference and inspiration for project managers looking to develop additional skills. Really, anyone who works with other people while executing tasks will find this book helpful.

Through everyday, recognizable situations and examples, this book covers insights and tools from over twenty-five years of project management. What follows are the observations and techniques from projects large and small, long and brief, complex and basic.

There is no particular profession, experience, or education level associated with what is presented here. Much of the content presented is the product of experiences from before my electrical engineering and MBA education. It was time I spent figuring out how to get things done, and that is a useful skill for anyone.

Project management is, in many ways, the same everywhere. Regardless of industry, location, or organization structure, similar, if not identical, project management skills are required. People are people, after all.

Many of the concepts and approaches shared here have a relationship to each other and have been organized accordingly.

Others are part of a constellation of tools and presented in loose groupings.

What is shared here is meant to be thought-provoking. The points presented may have more than one way of being interpreted. Feel free to jump around and read the sections you find most relevant. There is much to cover and take in. It took me more than 25 years to figure this all out.

Don't get overwhelmed. Developing project management skills is a journey. Be patient with yourself.

The Toolbox

Glossary of Terms

This glossary has been included here to establish a common understanding of the fundamentals.

People-centric – Focus on the human part of the equation. This does not include checklists nor software applications. Leveraging understanding of why and how people behave when executing tasks.

Project management phenomena – Repeating people, process, and project interactions not commonly understood but often universally recognized. The phenomenon (singular) / phenomena (plural) concept is woven into every part of this book.

The Matrix organization – An organizational philosophy where the hierarchy is flattened and related skills and resources are grouped together. This reduces cost and facilitates outsourcing.

N-1 and the stretch – A human resources philosophy implemented to increase productivity. The number of people to perform a task is identified. Then one is subtracted from that number (N-1). The attenuated team is then assigned the task. The goal is a "close enough" labor supply that the people "stretch" their efforts to cover the gap.

Most employers implement both the matrix and N-1 philosophies. Even smaller companies where these practices are not official policy do this.

Recommended Reading

The large number of phenomena presented in this book could be overwhelming if read start-to-finish. Perhaps the following phenomena read out of sequence could be considered a fast introduction.

It is all about communication
Building bridges
Speak the language
Credibility
Be positive
The self-organizing fallacy
Unleash the fury!
Constructive persistence

The Groundhog Day Experience of Project Management

Insanity is doing the same thing over and over and expecting different results.
– Albert Einstein

There is a movie called Groundhog Day, starring Bill Murray. The protagonist wakes up each morning to live the same day over and over. Even death cannot free him from his déjà vu existence.

The Groundhog Day experience of project management is the replaying of the same project-impacting phenomena, project after project. The predictable recurrence of events adding stress, cost, or delay. It's a déjà vu experience bordering on the pathological.

Reflexively, I began building a toolbox to address the observed phenomena.

Presented in this book is an array of project management phenomena common to almost all projects, regardless of subject or discipline. However, even just the common understanding they exist has never manifested. Everyone experiences the same challenges, but no one appears to be writing them down or really planning for them. For my own benefit, I began to record and standardize the situations and my strategies for successful resolution.

This development of a project management toolbox improved my effectiveness. Noticeably so. I eventually landed at an organization that valued achievement, innovation, and excellence, and these independently developed tools paid off.

What is my interpretation of the definition of project management? Project management happens whenever someone attempts a task in an organized manner. The ideas and concepts shared throughout the book are universally applicable and deliver value at all levels, for any project, helping you achieve that organization for success. From planning to rebuild your car's suspension on your non-work time to improving project teamwork within a global corporation.

Fundamentally, all projects exist to increase value. Resources and labor hours are organized as inputs, with a defined output chartered as the goal. Between those inputs and outputs is a vast interaction of human activity. People, communication, and process, this in-between space that is the focus of this book.

Now for stories giving insight to this book's genesis.

It is really not that intuitive

While attending a Society of Women Engineers (SWE) meeting, a colleague at least twenty years my junior and I went to lunch together. Project management was the first topic brought up. She talked about the confusion and frustration regarding the ever-changing priorities and the havoc it was having on her efforts.

Having already identified this as common project management phenomena, I shared the ABCDE concept detailed later in this book. Explaining that this is something that happens often in project management, I did a straightforward demonstration on a paper napkin. A short and to-the-point example.

My colleague appreciated the explanation, glad for the insight and confirmation she is not the only person seeing the problem. My colleague then requested to take a photo of my scribbles and thanked me for sharing.

It made me realize my observations about project management phenomena could be useful.

In another instance, a supervisor, after a year of managing my work, shared his observation that I have a certain set of street smarts for project management. He called it a workman-like approach effective in executing and completing projects. One colleague even started referring to me as the "sledgehammer" for my success in moving difficult projects forward. My toolbox was delivering tangible results—and real value.

Another colleague commented to me on my project management style. He pointed out that when I worked on a project, many of my actions did not make sense to an outside observer. Then at some point, everything would come together successfully at the end. The project reached its desired resolution, but the process was not clear to a casual observer.

These comments were the catalysts for exploring the "in-between" space, and they led me to the conclusion that I had developed a set of project management tools that, while recognized as effective, were not obvious to everyone else.

I wondered if I could develop a toolbox of project management tools that could help others. Would there be a benefit to writing down the background and explanations? Could synergies be created in a project management environment if everyone had access to the same toolbox?

My career is far from over, and putting the toolbox together increases my effectiveness, allowing for more tool development over time. Colleagues and my supervisor may gain additional insight into challenges we experience together. This book could increase the effectiveness of our collaboration. If we benefit from it in our project management work, then it will likely positively impact others who read it.

What we have here is a failure to communicate...

A particular challenge addressed with this text is the complexity of communicating project management phenomena. I have learned the hard way that the principles shared in this book can be difficult to express in conversation. The insights into project complexity are difficult to explain quickly, a likely scenario when deadlines are looming.

Shared frustration is the typical outcome when working through recurring project management phenomena that are paradoxically, not commonly understood. This drives the need for a record of concepts and situations that can be shared to create a common language. A reference which is this book's intent.

But because these communication principles are so challenging to get across, even reading about them is not enough. Still more is needed. That is why the concept of this book as a tool came about. It can and should be used to help improve project communication and execution. The physical copy of the book is an instrument to identify shared challenges in project management and provide a path to resolution. If two people have read this book, they can reference it when their shared project demonstrates one of the phenomena described.

This helps colleagues develop a common project management language for understanding complex project management phenomena. The book becomes a reference leading to straightforward resolution of project management phenomena and misunderstandings, improved engagement, and ultimately, better project delivery.

Without a common reference established ahead of time, people get caught up in the heat of the moment while experiencing project management phenomena and may arrive at different conclusions. Instead of a moment of shared understanding, the interaction may devolve into confrontation and conflict.

To aid in collaboration of book use, each chapter has a relatable title to make finding topics easier. With that, communication about difficult-to-explain project management phenomena can be more efficiently achieved.

No homework will be assigned

A variety of practical and applied approaches to project management are presented throughout. There will be no Gantt or Pert charts, nor formulaic spreadsheet tools. This book is checklist free.

There are, however, descriptions of phenomena for which a solution is elusive. Confirmation that they exist gives people something to consider and plan for.

There are also quotes scattered throughout the book. Collected over the years, I found them insightful and synergetic with the tools presented.

My sincere hope is what follows will benefit you as much as it has me.

CHAPTER 1

Communication is Fundamental

There are four ways, and only four ways, in which we have contact with the world. We are evaluated and classified by these four contacts: what we do, how we look, what we say, and how we say it.
– Dale Carnegie

The interpretation of this quote I subscribe to:

There are only four ways to know someone: By what they say, what they write, their appearance, and what they do.

Communication is the beginning and the end. The alpha and the omega. And everything in-between. Project management involves resources, planning, goals, deliverables, and more. All of this must be communicated. Verbally, in writing, and in person.

Without effective, strategic communication, a project manager will never reach their potential.

Then add the global environment to the equation. Long-term collaboration and relationships are often initiated and maintained without ever meeting in person. English as a second language, different cultures, and time zones all require communications with limited personal contact.

Verbal and written communications in today's hyperconnected workplace have multiple dimensions that need to be taken into account. It is not unusual to have a phone conversation or email exchange with someone, even a critical contributor, who has never (nor will ever) meet you in person. Your collaborative effort is executed exclusively through impersonal communications. A robust, polished communication capability will deliver superior project management outcomes.

What effort has gone into making your verbal or written communications effective? Have you ever solicited feedback on your phone style? Do you avoid starting most sentences in an email with "I"? Can you get to the point? Do you know when to stop speaking? Can you structure an email? Have you ever self-reflected on your communication capabilities and worked to improve them? The good news is that should you invest even a minimal effort, you will deliver noticeable improvement.

Awareness of the many dimensions in the communications space is important. Many nuances can be leveraged. Communication strategies often start as static, pre-planned efforts. As experience is developed, combining the different communication concepts further improves the likelihood of achieving the desired outcome. Eventually, proficiency develops to being comfortable with dynamic, real-time implementation of different approaches.

Communication is not just the mechanical act of transferring information through a chosen medium. The timing of the communication is important. As is using the right words, tone, who is included or excluded, whether you are notifying someone, transferring information, or prompting action.

Your demeanor and attitude will impact the effectiveness of your communication. A positive attitude, especially in the face of adversity, is a force multiplier in achieving your goals. Remaining consistently calm and positive demonstrates your maturity as a project manager.

Communication is a complex endeavor. Acknowledging this is a critical insight. Developing effective communication skills can only improve project management success. Some people are natural communicators. For the rest of us mere mortals, we have to work at it.

Welcome to the middle of everything

During a job interview the hiring manager brought up the subject of communication. I shared that as an application engineer much of what I did was to move information around. To be honest others did most the actual "work". One of the skills I would bring to this new role was expertise in being the go-between for information. Also, my experience engaging different people both vertically and laterally both inside and outside the organization. Being in the middle of everything was a familiar role.

Project management is a communicate, organize, and execute role. If we are honest with ourselves, others do most of the work.

Considering the array of talent and skill needed to achieve most anything worthwhile in a modern project, this makes sense. Marketing and sales know their jobs. As does engineering, quality, etc. In a project, a focal point tying all of these people and jobs together is required. Hence, there is a project manager.

Managing a project as the focal point is perhaps not all that different from being in senior management. Project management often interacts laterally and vertically within the organization. Your currency for achievement is information and influence. You're like a spider in the center of a web, managing information and communicating to deliver project success.

A project manager's primary skill is communication. A close second is analyzing information and being discriminative in its distribution. Project managers often act as a central clearinghouse for information, determining who needs to know what and when.

An oft-overlooked aspect of the information dimension is awareness of what should be shared with contributors to keep the project executing. Processing information is not a passive activity; it is more than just taking information and putting it places like a postal worker places letters in boxes. It is important to confirm accuracy, time criticality, distribution, and confidentially.

This management of information flow requires active engagement. An email from a senior manager may need to be rephrased and shared in a text or on a phone call. Information may need to be grouped until it reaches critical mass—or saved for a future request. A straightforward product-quality resolution may require face-to-face discussions with technicians who are finding the root of a problem. Or perhaps collaborating with Quality to create the document to share with the customer. Delivering messaging to sales who are demanding instant resolution.

Each of these groups will have a different focus and respond to different language. An array of communication skills will be needed. At some point, you may come to the conclusion, as I have, that communication is every bit as technical and complex as the technologies I studied to become an electrical engineer.

It is all about communication

Early in my career, I had an opportunity to visit customers in a role within the possibly most misunderstood of professions: sales.

Honestly, I had little respect for salespeople at the time. Perhaps other than an odd talent for finding the best restaurants, I could not justify their existence. This was the naïve, narrow world view of the left-brained, technically focused person I was at the time.

Then came the sales calls, and I experienced how tough sales really is. The strange thrill of cold calling. The development of relationships. The complexities of a supplier/customer interaction. From a front-row seat, I learned about communication and the importance of getting it right. I realized that the role of sales was more critical to organizational success than I had ever considered.

Sales communications are far more complex and challenging than I could have imagined. If you get it right, it is like having a superpower. Alternatively, communications that miss the mark could turn a difficult situation into a firestorm of failure.

Well-developed communication skills can turn a deteriorating situation into the building block of mutual future success—

especially when engaging different professions within an organization (engineering, purchasing, management, etc.).

Working with people in sales, whose careers live or die by their communication skills, clearly revealed my own anemic abilities in the space. Thus, I learned I needed to do better in the communication department.

People bring certain skills and experience to the work environment. It is why we are there. Compensation is largely tied to these characteristics. Our opportunities to contribute to the collective effort are determined by the bullet points on our résumés. Decades are spent building knowledge, skills, and experience. It's a continuous drumbeat of development.

Communication is an important learned skill and the force multiplier that facilitating your other hard-won skills, achieving their full potential.

Talking to people is an everyday requirement in project management. Phone calls, meetings, texts, emails, instant messaging ... so much communication. In my humble opinion, project management is more an exercise in communication and human interaction than it is in being proficient in whatever computer programs or tools your organization subscribes to.

When you're about to communicate with someone:

- Think about what you will say

- Think about what you will write

No one wants to read or listen to a meandering, unfocused statement or question.

- Say what you are going to say

- Deliver the planned message to the correct audience

- **And then stop.**

Communication is a tool serving a purpose, and like other tools, it must be used properly.

Communicate at the right time. In meetings, there is a benefit to waiting, letting others share first. This helps you better understand where the discussion is going so as to better focus your contribution. People have a need to communicate, and it is often best to let them talk and get it out before properly engaging. It is just part of the human equation.

Choose the right medium. Email works for many things, but voice is better, and in person is supreme. In person is the best way to engage in effective communications, and for introverts, this is tough to master. It was for me. But after spending a few years traveling with extroverted sales managers, I learned to talk to anyone, anywhere, anytime.

Consistency in communication is important. You need to speak and write in a repeatable way. Those who work with you need this predictability. Over time, the format of your communications will help others minimize the time needed to get the needed information.

Communication skills are the basic tools in your project management toolbox. It is likely you have many opportunities for improvement in this critical skill.

Building bridges

Cultivating relationships with colleagues throughout the organization is a necessary skill. And not just for a project manager involved in accomplishing tasks. All endeavors involve people.

People require relationships. For those who are left-brain dominant, the realization of the importance of this concept is perhaps similar to an alcoholic realizing they have a drinking problem.

"My name is Erik Lange, and I am left-brain dominant."

Even extroverts, who gain their energy from group participation, are not necessarily naturals at building bridges. Hanging out with and liking people are not the same as developing a professional relationship with work colleagues.

To survive, develop, and excel in the project management environment requires a network of colleagues providing support. Be prepared to engage both laterally and vertically within the organization (even outside the organization) when building bridges. Perhaps a key person in a different time zone is needed, or someone in shipping and receiving. Projects can have broad elements requiring enterprise-wide collaboration.

Bridge-building success will hinge on a singular characteristic: credibility. The more developed your reputation is as a good faith partner, the more likely others will engage for mutual success. Professional relationships are mutually beneficial. This is not a one-way engagement.

This is where polite and professional delivers. Be personable. Funny stories help. Being useful helps. Being able to present a mutually beneficial value proposition in a way that is easily understood makes a difference.

Building bridges eventually evolves to the next level: networking. Engage colleagues from across the organization. Organization networking is a next-level project management demonstration of skill. *Building bridges* writ large.

After reading all of this section, you may have come to the conclusion that building bridges is a calculating and manipulative approach.

Yes, it is.

Project management is all about planning, calculating, positioning resources, and leveraging every opportunity to achieve success—all while following the organization's policies and maintaining your integrity.

There is much focus on planning, process, and tools in project management. Determining the critical path, achieving on-time delivery, and delivering below budget are a few examples.

Make building bridges part of your sophisticated project management "people plan."

It cannot be emphasized enough how important bridge building is. This is a critical success factor for career development. Develop this skill until it is a reflex.

Words matter

After a successful sales call with an experienced and successful sales manager, he shared some profound advice. He said I should never use the word "simple." Use "straightforward" or even "basic," but never "simple." He continued by saying that if something is described as "simple" and the person being addressed does not understand immediately, you have insulted them for not understanding the "simple" concept.

Just because a word has a common meaning does not mean the situation-dependent interpretation of it will evoke the desired outcome.

An even more skilled approach is to avoid words that may be negatively interpreted and deliver a more collaborative message such as, "I think we may be able to solve the problem."

At the time of the sales manager's advice, I felt this idea about unintended word interpretation was over represented, but I kept myself open to the concept and observed word choices having impact. It took some time and consideration, but eventually this concept took root in my mind and has impacted my communications ever since.

Observe and practice to familiarize yourself with certain inflammatory words ("simple" is one). Then you can navigate around them. The effect of word choice in communications is often situation-dependent, and decisions need to be made dynamically during a conversation.

Sensitivity to word choices is important when developing a particular topic's messaging. Word selection and audience awareness will make the difference between a message influencing and a message missing the mark. This is why marketing and communications careers exist.

Again, awareness and practice will help develop this skill.

Forty-three seconds

Everyone reading these words has sat through a meeting where the presentation goes on and on. The message is neither succinct, nor focused. Time slows. The speaker overemphasizes tangential details, gets sidetracked, etc. Afterward, you are able to summarize in three sentences what was presented over forty minutes.

For communications in general, quantity is not quality. Eventually someone gave me insight into this better way.

While visiting customers with an experienced sales manager (same individual as in the *Words matter* example), an insight was shared that I have never forgotten. "Forty-three seconds," he said. "You only get forty-three seconds to deliver your message. Anything longer and you will lose them or what you are saying may not be interpreted in the way you intended."

Humans are not machines. Think about the message you are trying to land with your audience. Listening to you speak should not feel like an IQ test or an endurance event. Get to the point. Do not go off on tangents. Add no filler. Do not try to impress anyone with how smart you are. Just drill the information.

State the key points followed by a couple of sentences providing details, **then shut up.** My apologies for being blunt, but knowing when to stop talking is a skill. Acknowledge this, and build that ability to deliver a succinct message with a clear ending.

Forty-three seconds is a proper communication duration. Then be silent and wait for the reply.

Run silent, run deep

Silence is a powerful tool. Most people cannot stand periods of silence during a conversation. It is something that can be used for emphasis during a presentation and for persuasion when negotiating. Silence can move mountains if implemented correctly. Ask a question and go silent. Wait and wait if necessary. The answers will be forthcoming. This is another skill requiring practice. Once you nail this down, it feels like having a superpower.

When used in combination with *Forty-three seconds*, silence is amazing. Deliver your polished, thought-out, forty-three-second message, and then stop and wait. Your audience will respond, the silence prompting them to comment or ask questions.

So now you are fully aware of the value of silence. Others are also aware of the value of silence. Thus, there is a countermove to silence you should be aware of. Others may listen to what you are saying, and when you end and segue to silence, they answer your silence with silence.

They are seeing if, when confronted with silence, you will keep speaking to fill the void, potentially sharing more information than you intended. If you are truly finished speaking, then maintain your silence; if it drags on too long, ask if there are questions. Don't let people set you to babbling just because you cannot stand the silence.

Asking good questions

Asking questions is a superpower on par with the use of silence. Some questions are straightforward requests for defined information. The goal in these requests is a fast and efficient process for all parties involved. Other requests are more along the lines of troubleshooting. The goal is to solicit unknowns. This kind of question asking is different.

The profession of the question's recipient will impact how the question is structured. Engineers will interpret and respond differently than marketers. There are no hard and fast rules for navigating these engagements, other than being aware of the differences and that each communication is unique and dynamic.

To move your efforts forward, the goal is to look for valuable nuggets of information during each conversation.

Engineers are a great example of the complexities of question asking. Engineers know what they know. They are typically dedicated and proud of their profession, with knowledge hard won after many hours of study and execution.

Technical specialists with knowledge deep and wide, they are challenged answering questions from anyone outside their profession. Many of them gave up years ago explaining to the uninitiated what they do. It is not that they are unsocial or unwilling. Their understanding of specific technical environments is so rarified, that outside of a peer, it is unlikely anyone who asks a question regarding their specialty will ever understand.

This results in a weird situation if you need to ask questions of an engineer and they want to answer. But understanding each other is almost impossible. The question asker lacks the understanding to pose a proper question, and the engineer is challenged to provide an answer the listener can understand.

This is compounded by the fact that while engineers are remarkably proficient in the technical aspects of their profession (a left-brain activity), they are unlikely to have put much consideration into communicating this information (a right-brain activity).

Discovering and rendering into explanation this phenomenon could be one of my greatest accomplishments.

Be mindful of this situation when engaging experts. You think you are asking the right question, but to the listener of the question, what you are asking borders on nonsense. You may have to come at the question from different directions until you build a bridge of common understanding. This may feel like an IQ test combined with a patience marathon, but this skill too will improve with experience.

Then there are the questions soliciting an unknown. There are times you will ask a question and a colleague will state, "Just look it up on the internet or read the manual." Why might you need to ask them such a simple question?

Because there is context and experience needed for a proper answer. Things that are not written down. By asking the expert, you open the door to the possibility for a more complete and sophisticated answer than will be found on the internet or in a manual.

Asking questions is a skill that benefits from attention and proper development. Effort in this area delivers value.

Now can you explain it?

I had the opportunity to be an adjunct professor at my engineering school alma mater. They say you find out what you really know about a subject when you try to teach it. This became very apparent as I spent several hours in preparation for each hour of instruction. There was a lot to learn if I was going to teach.

Asking good questions is an important skill that leads to the next activity: explaining to or teaching others. Answering questions and explaining things is another skill everyone needs to work on.

Word choices, context, and completeness all need to be considered. On the other side, language skills, education, and experience of the recipient are important factors. My personal experience is that reviewing my explanation from the point of view of the other people involved is key.

Let's say that again. Consider your explanation from the viewpoint of the person you are communicating to.

In the instant message, email, and information-overload age we live in, incomplete communication is common. Ill-thought-out responses and rushed word choices deliver less than constructive outcomes.

In the international setting, explanations require genuine effort as English as a second language comes into play. Americans must stop using slang and pop culture references. Cease using vague, non-specific words such as "thing," "stuff," "sorta," etc. This topic will be emphasized later in this book.

Explanations are a skill to be developed. Time and money are saved by quality explanations. **Delivering an on-target message that resonates with the recipient, constitutes a complete answer, and does not require additional clarification is a beautiful thing.**

In person for maximum effect

The law of inverse ninja strength - The effectiveness of a group of ninjas is inversely proportional to the number of ninjas in the group.

Just as in the movies where groups of ninjas are wimps but individual ninjas are invincible, so does the effectiveness of communication increase as the number of people involved decreases. Maximum effectiveness is achieved at one-on-one.

People like myself, an introverted Myers-Briggs Type Indicator INTJ, are by nature not likely to engage others in person.

Approximately 40% of the population is introverted. Their natural inclination is to not even consider developing communication effectiveness. This is a challenge to be overcome. Fortunately, years of time working closely with extroverted salespeople taught me the value of speaking to people in person.

My first instinct now is to go speak to someone, in person. I have worked in places that employed many people who were very introverted. They are more comfortable with an email exchange than talking face-to-face. The look of shock exhibited by introverts when engaged in person is a common experience for me.

Verbal communication is the more influential than written— in-person verbal communication being the most effective approach. Phone communication is always better than written. Email is the worst for connecting and prompting action. Choose the channel based on the desired outcome for the communication effort.

Instead of falling back on email or instant messaging, pick up the phone and make that call. Walk over to their workspace and start up that conversation. Like all the other approaches shared here, this one requires practice.

Say thank you

Politeness has value. Saying thank you brings benefits to the project management environment. It demonstrates that you are paying attention and that you have empathy and commitment colleagues will appreciate.

A thank you also acknowledges the communication, closing the loop that the message was received. Open-ended communication in the modern work environment is a pervasive challenge. The assumption that the receiver received the message, knows about it, and the contents have value is not valid without a confirmation. A two-word reply of "thank you" confirms all those assumptions. This makes for a tighter and more effective communication environment.

Take advantage of old-fashioned politeness. Make this part of your positive communication style.

Opportunity for improvement

Now we know, and knowing is half the battle.
– GI Joe

Hopefully the message about the value of communication in project management has been delivered. Effective communicators and communication do not spontaneously occur. They begin with the understanding that success in any effort is subject to expertise in writing and speaking.

Another phenomenon you may find interesting: Efforts improving communication capability makes everyone involved more successful.

But wait, there's more ...

Nested inside the communication phenomenon is another phenomenon. That is almost no cost to improving communication. Just a little time, some mental bandwidth, reading this book, etc. No capital equipment cost. No monthly subscription. All that is needed is the willingness to self-evaluate, improve and maybe accept some input from colleagues and mentors.

Communication is a skill and a craft. Accepting this is not a "simple" topic and in many ways a technical endeavor.

Work at building your communication skills. The results will speak for themselves.

CHAPTER 2

Communication Complexity

The United States and Great Britain are two
countries separated by a common language.
– George Bernard Shaw

The English were possibly the most prolific explorers, colonizers, conquerors, and traders in world history. The result is English becoming the de facto global language for communication. If the English had not built an empire on which the sun never set, it is likely the global business environment would still be trying to agree on what language everyone will use.

Even with agreement on a common language, there are other factors to effective communication, including true understanding. Culture, profession, native language, nationality, even organizational eccentricities influence how words and concepts are interpreted. If both parties are not aligned on word meanings and inference, all sorts of unconstructive things happen.

Professions have their own terminology and often a somewhat unique worldview. Even their own language, if you will. To help yourself in these professions, learn that terminology, learn that worldview. It helps to at least have a surface understanding of the profession's communication nuances.

Different personalities find certain career choices appealing. This is not a perfect generalization, but it definitely meets the 80/20 rule threshold. Likely, more than 80% of the personalities in a chosen profession will have predictable characteristics.

The profession and personality combination provide a framework for improved communication. Take the time to investigate and understand this opportunity. Note how the participants communicate, the words they use, and what they value.

Someone in sales looks at earned revenue very differently from an accountant in finance. Management focuses on top- and bottom-line performance. Sales cares not one whit about the bottom line; they are incentivized on top line. Neither the top line nor bottom line is considered important by most engineers.

Working in the international arena introduces numerous language characteristics that impact communication. Communicating with someone who thinks in a language other than the one being spoken is different than communicating with a native speaker. Project management efforts will benefit from skills taking these added complexities into account.

The initial effort in figuring this out is difficult, but the value brought to your project management efforts is significant.

The pre-meeting meeting

An activity that is perhaps not so unusual but took me some time to understand was the management penchant for the pre-meeting. Whenever a meeting was planned, key participants would huddle beforehand to discuss their strategy. At the time, it seemed a needless amount of over-communicating. They already planned to attend a meeting on that exact subject. Why double the meeting time?

Since that experience, I have come to embrace the pre-meeting meeting.

The pre-meeting meeting can give you a chance to iron out any potential wrinkles. Perhaps it is a good idea to double-check a question with a colleague before putting them on the spot in front of your leadership. If confirmation from a colleague is expected while you are presenting, you should make sure they are on board with the message ahead of time. Key people need their input included ahead of time.

It's also an opportunity to align with your supervisor on a controversial topic before delivering the message in a setting where there is less control. If the meeting has political ramifications, there may be more than one pre-meeting meetings.

This activity does increase workload, but the return on investment for this time is very high. Especially if developing a uniform lock-step approach with leadership's vision is important to you.

With the pre-meeting done, the actual meeting will just be a public confirmation of what has already been discussed and decided. The participants' comfort level will be higher and the possibility of an unknown unexpectedly derailing the meeting will be greatly reduced.

Once you start on the path to embracing the pre-meeting meeting, likely you will not be able to go back.

Speak the language

There is a Bible story about an attempt to build a tower to heaven (the Tower of Babel). God eventually casts the tower down, simultaneously dooming humanity to speak many languages instead of one so as to prevent this heaven-reaching attempt from ever happening again. Communicating in the modern work environment often feels like the delivery of this judgment. So many professions and specialties. Each with unique jargon or terminology.

Approaching and engaging finance the same way you would engineering (or any other company department) is not a winning approach. Most professions see themselves as first among equals. We picked our professions and dedicated years to achieving within them. The very act of choosing your profession indicates you perceive it as the optimal choice. Otherwise, why did you push yourself to get where you are?

Thinking in a profession-centered way is neither constructive nor success-inducing. Respecting other professions and their contributions to the collective effort is a necessity. A level of self-awareness in this space must be developed ... unless your ego prevents you from considering other professions worthy. A respectful attitude cannot be faked in this situation. If you do not respect others and/or their profession, it will become evident in your interactions.

Personally, I am often in awe of my colleagues' skills. Many of them have talents I lack. By developing this understanding, you are better able to integrate these people and their talents into your projects. The more adept you become at this, the more sophisticated and effective your project management efforts become.

My employer tasked me with managing the North American marketing and communications efforts. This had me working with a proper marketing firm on advertising, trade shows, publications, and announcements.

The marketing firm's people were talented and competent. One particular experience stands out. The account manager contacted me for input on something with significant artistic content. He wondered if I thought what had been shared looked acceptable.

How would I know? I am an electrical engineer without an artistic bone in my body. My personal crowning artistic achievement in understanding colors is to not wear grey and tan together.

My recalled response: "You're asking me? I do not have the fundamental talent, much less any skill to be able to provide a useful opinion. This is your area of expertise. What is your call on this?"

My understanding of the ask was sufficient to realize the firm should rely on others more skilled for input.

This concept applies to professions and corporate culture. Also to interactions with management and leadership. We'll get to more on the management angle in a later chapter.

Project management will have you interacting with other professions and groups within the organization. Engineers talk to marketing people. Accountants in finance collaborate with business professionals on budgets.

Each of these professions has different professional languages. Accountants and engineers tend to be structured and introverted. Marketers and salespeople are more extroverted and organizationally creative. They value different things. Learn what these things are. Walk a mile in their shoes, so to speak. Use the words they value when speaking to them. Even the smallest amount of this insight will go a long way toward improving project execution when contributors are needed from different backgrounds.

In addition to learning how to better engage colleagues while taking into consideration the unique language of their chosen profession, it is important to not inflict your chosen profession's more eccentric approaches to communication. Adapt your language depending on the audience. It can help prevent painful misunderstandings.

Is this fair? I have to learn the eccentricities of corporate culture, department engagement, and unique professional communication approaches. And I need to remain positive and demonstrate forward motion to management All while not inflicting the peculiarities of my chosen profession on others.

No, it is not fair. This does not matter, because it is the way it is. Get over it.

Often, projects include broad lateral and vertical elements. Negotiating this labyrinth requires sophisticated and professional communication skills. Project managers will likely interact with different professions, skills, experience, and levels of engagement. Subject-matter experts with a high degree of skill in a unique specialty may be involved. This spectrum of partners requires skill and sensitivity to engage successfully. Organizing and executing a project across departments and involving different professions requires a practical and practiced approach.

Hence, there comes the need to develop the skills and practice engaging the Tower of Babel that is project management.

International communications

The phenomena and tools presented throughout this book are universally applicable. These are not American or English-speaking phenomena. They are human phenomena. It is almost comical how the differences in language, culture, and life experience can be almost insurmountable in some ways. But in other ways, similarities indicate a singular point of understanding. Project management is one of those singularities.

Today, even small companies have international interactions. Projects involve participants in other countries for whom English is a second language. English as a second language (ESL) adds variables to the communication equation. Learn how to exclude slang from your professional speaking and writing. Speak more slowly, and enunciate more clearly. This is a skill that requires practice. Emails must be uniformly structured. Project participants from outside the USA for whom ESL applies should not be picking through massive paragraphs or poorly structured explanations. **If you cannot organize an email, how can you be expected to organize a project?**

Without effective communication, your project management efforts will be challenged at best.

Here's an example: An American customer purchases a product from a European company, but the product is manufactured in Asia. The players: American customer, American sales manager, European management, two Asian manufacturing sites in two different countries with an antagonistic history toward each other.

A product update is required. The East Coast sales manager is on a rampage demanding instant results. For cultural reasons, the Asian participants refuse to communicate with each other. European management is concerned about the potential loss of business.

You realize that any eventual success in this situation will be delivered through communication. Not by technology or following procedure and process. If ever there was an argument to travel and meet colleagues globally, this project is it.

I was the go-between for my antagonistic Asian colleagues. Acting as the communications hub (*Welcome to the middle of everything*), all information was filtered through me (*It is all about communication*) and scrubbed of any reference to the other involved party. It involved carefully crafted emails and properly timed phone calls (*Now can you explain it?*). I kept everyone talking and delivered regular updates, all while talking the sales manager down from initiating corporate Armageddon. There was nothing glamorous or fun about it, just straightforward engagement and communications.

Perhaps this is a phenomenon nested inside another phenomenon. When meeting someone in the international space there is often a brief exchange of information. This initial short conversation is an acknowledgement of the geographical, national, and cultural differences.

This is the acknowledgement of the elephant in the room that we each have very different life experiences. Time zone differences or different holidays. I do not know why this happens. It is important to building a relationship with international colleagues.

Constructive acknowledgement of cultural differences early in your international communication efforts is a technique for quickly establishing a collaborative relationship.

I have a story I have shared with colleagues all over the world to help build a bridge to the human side. It's about when my uncle, an immigrant from Wales, began dating my father's sister. An invitation for dinner at my grandfather's home had been extended, and my uncle was to meet with the father of the woman he intended to court. A proper educated gentleman, he dressed in a London-made tailored suit and presented himself at the door.

This was in Wisconsin in the 1960s ...

My father answered the door. In a wife-beater and jeans. His father was sitting at the kitchen table, dressed the same.

The family assembled for dinner. The fall season had just begun, and the Wisconsin staple of sweet corn on the cob was served. A platter of steaming yellow corn. Which everyone eats using their hands ...

My future uncle watched all of this in horror. Who are these savages? In Wales, corn on the cob is what you feed pigs. You also do not eat with your hands.

He and my aunt have been married now for over 50 years.

My telling of his story of cultural differences resonates with those who regularly engage colleagues over the world. Sharing this early in the professional relationship develops the mutual understanding that you are aware of cultural differences. The self-deprecating nature of the story also delivers the message that I am not culture or ethno-centric. This story prevents misunderstandings from ever occurring.

Depending on where you are in the world, things work differently from in the United States. Risk tolerance, hierarchy, communication etiquette (politeness), and education rigor are examples of where a misalignment of understanding can deliver unexpected outcomes.

Risk tolerance can be low to virtually non-existent in some cultures and nationalities. If something is not clearly written down and official, it will not happen. This will impact your project management efforts.

The low risk tolerance of international colleagues is an eternal source of frustration for Americans. The concept of operating "outside the box" or "just make it work" is a non-starter for much of the world.

Also, hierarchy is crucial for most everyone outside the U.S. Again, Americans do not understand this. As an example, did you copy the person you are requesting information from in an email to their superior? No? Then there will never be a response. If their boss is not explicitly involved, it will never happen. This took some time for me to understand.

Americans are remarkably ignorant of formality. This is a broad generalization, but when I travel internationally, I am struck by how many interactions follow a set of rules commonly known and practiced.

Politeness is important for many. Many cultures require politeness. A "thank you" goes a long way. Phone etiquette will be important. The rude American stereotype is justified. I have worked with Americans permanently banned from any communication with colleagues in certain nations.

In Europe, workdays and meetings begin with a greeting of all your colleagues For Americans, that is a lot of touching and interaction. When I start my workday, I get two hours of continuous work completed before taking a short break and saying hello.

The biggest in-person culture-shock moment for many is regarding personal space. As an American, the first time European and Asian colleagues move in close while talking takes getting used to. It is funny watching the new American employees experiencing this for the first time. The American steps back for more comfortable personal space. The European colleague steps forward into a space they are comfortable with. The American is literally being chased around the room.

It is problematic to approach international communications from the simplistic viewpoint that if both parties speak English, everyone will understand each other. There is a complexity to international communications. Acknowledgment and skill development in this space is necessary for success.

But it is not the same English

A colleague from France is in the USA for a week of joint sales calls. We meet up on the East Coast, and while picking up the rental car, he specifies the navigation device be set to French because he will be driving.

As we are traveling down the highway, the GPS says something in French. Seconds later, my colleague glances my way and asks, "Is this the exit?"

How would I know? I don't speak French.

A common language is important.

Keep in mind, however, that even with English, Americans speak American English. The rest of the world has been educated in British English. This can lead to misunderstandings

It is safe to say that all education outside the USA is superior at teaching the Brits' proper English. I have sat in meetings where my Korean colleague next to me was correcting my grammar. International professionals take their English seriously and most likely conform to proper English norms.

There is another layer of complexity to the international communication using English as a common language. The individuals participating organize their thoughts in their native language. They are likely speaking English while following their native language's structure.

I have an example. An American colleague was frustrated while working with an eastern European colleague who was in turn interacting with a southern European supplier. My American colleague could not understand what they were saying even though it was all in English words. Sentence structure and word emphasis was different for each group. If someone did not mentally engage an international English filter and translate, no one was ever going to figure out what was being said.

To clarify communications, use basic wording, simplify sentence structure, and keep word counts to a minimum. Arriving at a common understanding requires a sophisticated understanding of the situation that is delivered in an uncomplicated way.

Remember to stick with the basics. Use words common to international English. These are found in your international colleagues' communications. Eventually, you begin to home in on words everyone in the world understands. The same with sentence structure. Through observation and practice, a common style emerges that is universally understood.

American irreverence is useful

Americans . . . you can teach them nothing.
– French colleague

There are opportunities in the international environment when American impertinence, high risk tolerance, willingness to think outside the box, and obliviousness to hierarchy is useful. There may be questions that need asking or people to be included, and hierarchical cultural complexities obstruct finding the path forward.

Your international colleagues will think, "Thank God the Americans are here. They will talk to anyone, regardless of position." Americans are just that way. It is almost impossible for most Americans to comprehend the hierarchy found in other countries. This is not being represented here as a criticism. I appreciate the advantages of being provincial.

Involving an American who can constructively engage different parties and resolve project challenges can inject efficiency into situations where nationality and cultural impacts on project execution are a challenge.

Word to the wise here: This is not a license to be stupid. Be respectful of your colleagues and sensitive to pushing too hard. A developed skill for politeness is required. If you do not understand what was just shared in this section, then you are not ready for this approach.

Things best left unsaid

Application engineers often find themselves working between internal engineering and sales. This in-between status often includes awareness of technical details or sensitive internal information that would be problematic to share with sales. This is a judgment call application engineers become more comfortable making with experience.

Developing a sensitivity recognizing when something is ready to be customer facing. Internal communications detailing a quality issue, product strategy, even just rumors and speculation will be interpreted through the "application engineer filter". In just seconds, the conclusion "sales will never see this" is made. Without this filter, bad things happen.

This application engineer filter is similar to the "confidential" filter. Recognizing internal-only information versus information that can be customer facing is an important skill. The next level is genuinely sensitive confidential information. Understanding these distinctions and their legal implications is important.

Compartmentalizing information should only happen if it is truly business-sensitive. My suggestion is to distribute as much information as broadly within the project participants as possible. Nothing is held back unless it could be interpreted as inflammatory or there are legal implications.

There are occasions where information needs to be shared, just not in writing. The only channel for this is verbal. Face-to-face or on a call. This is likely for a politically sensitive topic. **Remember: Emails are forever.**

This skill in sharing broadly, while still being judicious, is good to develop in its own right. An additional benefit is others will see the care with which you handle information. This opens the possibility of others also being willing to share their insights with you.

When executed well, having skills around information compartmentalization, judicious distribution, and recognizing information sensitivity= increase project efficiency and overall effectiveness.

Be very nice to the receptionist

My mother told me this when I was very young: Be nice to the secretary. Now we call them office assistants or office managers or whatever. Regardless, this advice is pure truth.

During your project management people engagements, be aware that, whether it's the receptionist or someone else, you may be talking to someone who has connections throughout the company. These connections do not show up on the org chart. Just because a colleague or project contributor did not climb the ladder does not mean they do not have a relationship with those who have. Gossiping or insinuation can have consequences.

Many receptionists or office managers are the nexus for information and wield influential power. They have unspoken alliances best not crossed. Additionally, the boss will be protective of this person. One wrong word and the world catches on fire.

Just as poor behavior can have a negative impact, so too can good behavior get a nod from the right person.

Finger on the scale

This chapter built on the previous chapter regarding how communication sophistication is critical to project management success. Awareness of specific, complex, phenomena and the skills needed.

The combined number of phenomena presented in chapters one and two is more than a dozen. Developing expertise in each one will have noticeable value. Once that phenomenon specific ability has been developed then the next opportunity presents itself. Leveraging synergistic combinations of phenomena skills.

Meetings are a universal opportunity for everyone. At the organization level, the team level, and as individuals, there is an opportunity for continuous improvement. Meetings have direct labor costs that can be reduced and opportunity costs to manage.

The international aspect could be a book in its own right. What is shared here is just the phenomena observed as common to project management. This along with the complexities of English as a second language, likely will give the reader several new approaches and opportunities to develop new skills.

Each phenomenon represents the option to put a finger on the scale and improve project management outcomes.

CHAPTER 3

Reducing Project Friction

A sophisticated expertise in communication is the superpower every project manager should aspire to develop. Acknowledging communications phenomena, and the benefits realized from skills addressing them, is important. Self-reflection, mentor and colleague input, and of course, practice, will develop your communication skills.

But wait, there's more ...

The foundation communication skills rest on is something I do not believe many consider as important to project management or communications in general.

I am speaking of credibility.

Credibility

Difficult and time consuming to establish, credibility makes the difference between effortless, high-efficiency project execution and the death march experienced by those less trusted.

Credibility makes everything so much easier. From credibility flows trust. Trust delivers that honest collaboration needed to move quickly and efficiently. Credibility and trust are the secrets to reducing friction in project execution.

A project manager without credibility is limited in the what, the how, and how fast. Meaning, the kinds of projects they are able to manage, how the projects are executed, and the speed of project progression.

Where does credibility come from? Integrity combined with predictability in personality and action. It is not just a function of following rules as written. If you demonstrate sociopathic behavior—or your actions foster the perception you are not a good-faith partner—your credibility is destroyed.

This is about more than being technically correct or demonstrating skill in executing an organized project. Do you finish what you start? Is what you say also what you do? Are you aware of the political ramifications of the project? Do you regularly deliver on schedule? Most importantly, when things go wrong—and they will—do you know when to give your colleagues and leadership the heads up and request assistance before the situation turns into a disaster?

If no one knows who you are, getting buy-in from contributors will be more challenging. A lack of credibility is especially difficult for new hires thrust into the project management role. They lack the history to establish credibility.

Credibility is a precious thing to be cultivated and jealously guarded. Once lost, credibility is almost impossible to get back. Those working in sales know this universal truth. They live or die on their credibility and zealously protect it. Keep the maintenance of your credibility in mind as you develop your project management footprint.

Attitude is everything

Project management can be a never-ending source of frustration. Why does it need to be this difficult ... every single time? Perhaps one thing to keep in mind is that any project of value will be challenging. **If this were easy, everyone would be doing it.** Make an effort to stay positive. It will distinguish you as a project leader, and those who participate in your projects should find it a positive experience.

In relation to positivity, note that insinuation is forbidden. This is an official company position at one of my previous employers. Insinuation is poison to an organization. If the facts are not in evidence, never insinuate. We all know who the dishonest backstabbing slackers are. Do not gossip about it. Never speak negatively of your colleagues. If you suggest something inappropriate and without proof, it will come back to haunt you.

Attitude overall is important to the success of every project. Be polite, be professional, stay positive, *Say thank you.* Solicit feedback from members of the project team.

Remain calm even when the inferno is raging around you.

Keeping calm can be very challenging. Many people reading this book are highly motivated type A personalities and unafraid of conflict. If the other party is throwing verbal attacks and engaging in passive-aggressive shenanigans, then turnabout is fair play? No, it is not. Regardless, resist the temptation, and remain a beacon of stoic professionalism.

By staying professional and engaged, the leader and the problem become obvious. Then let management or even peer pressure solve your problem for you.

If you lose your head and your focus while navigating the human problems of a project, you are not likely to succeed. Project management is a formidable activity providing a never-ending stream of irrational challenges. Start working on your calm demeanor.

It takes time and dedication, but this approach becomes self-reinforcing. It is also respected by senior management. This helps when you need to reach out to leadership for support in moving your project forward. They will have labeled you as a good-faith partner (*Credibility*) that they are willing to support.

Develop your attitude "A" game. You will need it.

Integrity

Demonstrating integrity in your activities can only help you in managing a project and in your relations with your superiors.

Early in my adult working life, I had my integrity tested. This is my response to that interview question, "Give an example of a time where you had to make a decision demonstrating integrity."

Having just returned from Army Reserve training, I began a job as a factory mechanic. Roll-away toolbox, tool belt, and all. It was a good job. I learned a lot and accomplished some fascinating things.

My supervisor was an accomplished person. He could thread pipe, run conduit, wire up a machine, weld, everything. For any skilled task performed in a factory, he was more than proficient. He was also a good teacher and would take the time to get you to the limits of your personal talent.

He was also a Vietnam combat veteran. Two purple hearts, one for being shot. The other for shrapnel in a mortar attack that scarred his face for life.

He was a good boss, but if you crossed him, God help you. Life had been rough on him, and he was mean. Junkyard-dog mean. And he had killed people (in Vietnam, at least).

After almost a year in my role, he called me out into the parking lot. The general manager was transferring to a new role, and his leased vehicle needed to be returned. My boss wanted me to pop open the dash and try to roll back the odometer.

Here is the part where integrity was tested.

I declined, because turning back the odometer is illegal.

Most people would say that refusing him was not too hard.

Really? The guy I refused did all the company terminations, has been shot before, and had killed human beings. Honestly, I wonder if I was in my right mind for saying no. You do not tug on Superman's cape, you do not pull the mask off the Lone Ranger, and telling this guy no gets you fired.

He did not fire me. He was okay with me saying no. I think I may have even earned some respect from him that day.

Most employers have integrity training telling you to do the right thing, blah blah blah. But when integrity is really needed, it will be sorely tested. If you can pull off integrity without triggering a bad outcome you have a bright future ahead.

Most people will not have such severe integrity tests. The challenge appears to be in recognizing when situations requiring good judgment occur. In the rush to find the most efficient path to delivering, you may cross a line without knowing it.

Never make it up

Application engineering is one of the best roles an engineer can have. Not best in terms of money or upward mobility, but best in terms of low stress, if you have what it takes. When a sales manager needed me, they would set up the customer visits, tell me when and where to book tickets to and from, which hotels I would stay in and on what day. I would literally fly in, walk out of the terminal, and the sales manager would pick me up and drive me from place to place. Even the restaurants for lunch and dinner were chosen for me.

During the customer visits, the sales manager did most of the talking. It was that easy. All the uninteresting details are handled by others. Perhaps that is what being a celebrity is like.

Then, at some point in the sales meeting, one of the customer's experts would turn to me and ask a series of questions related to the product we were selling. The person(s) asking the question(s) were typically twenty-five-year-plus subject-matter-expert veterans with hardcore experience in their field. They do not ask questions like what color the product is. Their questions were rocket scientist–challenge level.

For me to keep my job, the expectation was for me to answer 90% of those questions when they were asked. For the other 10%, I could beg for time to gather more information.

This is a high-pressure situation. The sales manager watches to make sure you do not damage a customer relationship years in the making. The customer's technical experts need correct answers and will know the difference. You must deliver now and deliver real value.

Once you deliver the answer, you can look forward to the end of the sales call and a nice lunch or dinner.

If you can deliver.

The moral of the story is these situations will happen, and you need to be able recognize them and have a strategy. All this while avoiding panicking, not spooking the customer, and not making factually false statements.

Similar high-pressure situations abound in project management. They are semi-confrontational gotcha situations where questions are asked with the expectation of an immediate, complete, and accurate response.

Making up an answer for convenience or to end a pressure situation is the same as telling a lie. Nothing crashes your credibility like being caught in a lie. Getting back lost credibility is almost impossible. Something earned from years of effort can be lost in minutes.

There are roles and situations where you are asked questions. Difficult questions. By customers, sales managers, engineers, etc. They can come from many sources. Your boss or more senior management, for example.

When this happens, the foremost thought in your mind should be the understanding that what you say has real-world ramifications. A customer's application could fail. The sales manager you support could be denied the sale. Internal development could act on your statement and cause the project to deliver garbage. There is political pressure for a fast and complete response.

Yet, it certainly would be much easier to just say what they want to hear.

Don't do it.

Learn to recognize these situations. Stay calm. Develop a strategy for when you do not know the answer. A practiced, polished response to provide an update in 24 hours is better received than a flustered, fumbling on-the-fly attempt to provide an immediate and possibly incorrect answer.

Have a plan, and never make things up.

Close the loop

An executive manager at one of my previous employers had the best follow-up game of anyone I have ever worked with. And I have been emulating him ever since.

No matter who you were in the company, from top to bottom, if you asked him a question, he would get you the answer. Sometime within two weeks, the answer would be delivered by phone, or show up in an email, or in some cases someone else would provide the answer after the question was passed to them.

This follow-up reliability reduced everyone's stress. There is nothing fun about pinging an executive for follow-up on a question they agreed to answer. My mentor on this delivered every single time. This reliable delivery over time builds rock-solid credibility.

Always follow up if at all possible. My follow-up list is so long I write things down to keep track. There are times when two weeks have gone by and I deliver the follow-up and I can hear the surprise on the phone. They thought you had forgotten. They will also never forget you delivered.

Never ASSUME, because when you ASSUME,
you make an ASS of U and ME.

–Anon

The follow-up concept also applies to closing the loop on communications. Do not assume the other parties "got it." Be explicit. "I apologize for double-checking on what is probably commonly understood, but is xx planned?" In today's world of communication overload, details can be overlooked or the messaging was of poor quality and a follow-up delivers needed alignment.

From a credibility standpoint, the best follow-up is in-person (*In person for maximum effect*), with by phone being second. Email is the lowest quality of follow-up, but in many cases, email is appropriate. For those tough follow-ups, call or meet in person. This builds credibility by showing you are a good-faith partner who cares enough to deliver the message verbally.

Solid follow-up execution builds credibility and drives project success.

Follow up, close the loop. Learn it, live it.

Deliver or notify

Delays happen. Sometimes they happen often and for reasons beyond our control.

It is a difficult position when what you are managing is really needed but you can only deliver delay messages instead of the final deliverables. Regardless, keep everyone involved updated. Make the call— voice is better, in person is best (*In person for maximum effect, Close the loop*). Keep the stakeholders informed. A few of them may grumble, but in the end, your updates only increase your credibility.

If someone is expecting a reply and you are still waiting for the information to pass along, let them know you are working on it. Also acknowledge any update requests regarding delays in work or delivery. Staying connected demonstrates competence.

Over time, this will turn into a sixth sense, a little voice telling you an update is due (or past due). You have mastered this skill when you deliver an update and they say, "I was just about to call you about this."

Perform due diligence

Due diligence is about gathering information before taking action. Figuring things out, filling in the blanks, confirming requests, etc.

Did I first do everything I could to figure this out on my own? Completely read an email before responding? Try finding the answer in the company literature before asking a colleague? Being able to figure things out, especially the easy stuff, without engaging others helps your credibility.

Due diligence applies to communications. Are you sure of your response? Really sure? Who is the audience? If you are in error, will it be considered inflammatory? If several levels of management above you are copied on the email, you will want to double or even triple check. Maybe have a colleague read it over.

There is no such thing as perfect understanding, but have you done what is reasonable? And then have you double-checked to make sure a simple mistake does not derail your effort?

Expertise in due diligence is important to developing and maintaining credibility. The goal is not perfection. Just a solid effort to show that you are paying attention.

Allies

You will need alliance-building skills to succeed in project management. This is not about engaging contributors in a project. Allies are those who share information, look out for your interests, and are willing to support your project management activities.

Allies are critical in bringing groups together. Mediating misunderstandings. Making introductions and sharing of credibility credentials between strangers. "Bob gave me your name as someone I should reach out to," etc.

Recognizing the need for allies and how to engage them is another of those important skill sets every project manager needs.

Mentors

Part of developing as a project manager is learning where your skills, talents, and gaps are. Much of this will come from your own internal review. Another equal or greater contributor to your quest for professional growth will come from mentors.

There are limits to self-reflective improvement. This is when having a mentor helps. Mentors provide those honest conversations needed to fully develop your potential. They can help make sense of experiences you do not understand or give insight into management's motivations and actions. They watch your performance and provide feedback. A good mentor will anticipate pitfalls and share what is needed for you to be successful.

Most mentoring interactions will be fairly straightforward. For instance, they'll point out your gaps, how you've improved, safe topics, safe feedback, etc.

Your mentor/mentee relationship hits a deeper level when ruthless, brutal honesty is shared. The mentor must be experienced and genuinely supportive of your self-interest. It helps if you as a person are able to accept someone holding up a mirror showing your opportunities for improvement. This is the space where the heavy-lifting of self-improvement will occur. Just because you think you are ready for this level of soul-shriveling self-revelation does not mean you are. You have been warned.

The understanding of the need for a mentor, figuring out who they are, and then building a working relationship with that person is a worthy goal for every project manager.

Making the sausage

Writing things down is important. Lists of useful information. Notes on ideas. Rough drafts that are works in progress.

Any written creation has two elements of energy put into it. The rough original layout with all the concepts, comments, and ideas is the first. The second part of the energy is the polish of the materials for greater distribution. These are not typically equal levels of expended energy.

The in-process documents are the making of the sausage. For the most part, they are not ready for others to see. All the good elements are included, but it is not pretty. However, these rough drafts are efficient and conserve energy. Everything is there if you are willing to overlook the aesthetics. With rough drafts, you've accomplished 80% of the value with 20% of the energy.

I personally operate almost completely in rough materials right up until something is needed for greater distribution. Then a final polish is performed. This conserves energy and allows me to accomplish more.

A scenario that comes up: Someone asks me for what I have. The latest version of a presentation. A rough draft of a document. Notes from a recent meeting. I send over my rough draft/notes with a comment that this is not a polished final document, but all the information is there. When sharing documents like this, it is important to put a disclaimer up front. Rough Draft! Not Ready for Distribution!

The scenario that often plays out is after receiving this pre-polished version, the requestor comments on the rough state of what you sent. More polish would have been appropriate since this was shared with more senior managers.

They were drafts! You shared what was available and declared them drafts beforehand.

Avoiding this misuse scenario will take some practice, but maximizing documentation creation while minimizing energy consumed is a force multiplier in your project management efforts.

The making the sausage approach is a way to increase your throughput by avoiding the finalizing/polishing time sink unless you absolutely must make those changes. Just remember to tell those you work with about your approach to prevent misunderstandings.

High speed, low drag

This is the chapter that explains why some project managers seem to effortlessly execute through difficult projects while others have to act as a battering ram for each step of progress. Credibility being the secret to success in reducing project execution friction.

The credibility part is often less understood. In why it is important, how it impacts project execution, and how to achieve and maintain it. A self-assessment combined with input from a mentor is important in your credibility journey.

Credibility is needed to deliver success in engaging Allies to further improve your project management portfolio.

Communication and credibility work together. Several communication related phenomena impacting credibility were introduced in this chapter (*Never make it up, Close the loop, Deliver or notify, Perform due diligence*). The communication skills addressing phenomena in earlier chapters are the building blocks for executing these new approaches.

Making the sausage is a minimalist skill idea for freeing up energy. Creating a space where less polished information can be presented with the understanding it is for educational purposes only and not ready for distribution.

Credibility comes with experience. Acknowledge this phenomena and work towards building yours.

CHAPTER 4

Engaging Management for Success

Nowhere does *Speak the language* apply more than when communicating with management. Interacting with higher levels of supervision benefits from speaking- and writing-skill development in profound ways. Appropriate word use, emphasis, attitude, and credibility become imperative.

Poorly worded, incomplete, and inaccurate emails demonstrate your limitations to management. Droning on about the topic under discussion does not make you look smart nor show you as a thought leader. Concise and to the point is the goal (*Forty-three seconds*). Demonstrate that you understand their time is valuable and have made efforts to conserve your use of it.

Communicating with more senior members of the organization requires an additional shift in the language used. It is deadly important that what is said or written is accurate (*Perform due diligence*), shows teamwork, is positive, and delivers solutions. Senior and executive management are always inspecting the team for effective collaboration, inclusive communication, and constructive paths forward. And they remember every detail.

Despite what is said about open doors and being there to hear your complaints, management is not interested in your negativity. There is a distinct difference between identifying gaps and presenting constructive solutions versus being a complaining whiner. Learn that difference.

Identifying genuine challenges is a valuable skill. Complaining, insinuating, grumping, and venting are examples of skills that have no value. Every manager is presented with a never-ending stream of challenges. They all develop a technique of classifying, organizing, delegating, and then dealing with the most relevant challenges.

Can you help management achieve their goals without making things worse? Without burning bridges? Without forcing the leadership to micromanage? Can you be trusted with responsibility?

These are questions to be considered in your journey to improve as a project manager.

Be positive

Didn't we just talk about attitude in the previous chapter? Yes. And this concept is important enough to appear twice.

Whining and complaining to management is not a strategy for success. Your leadership is not a surrogate set of parents who tolerate your poor behavior. Additionally, managers have a high gain setting. Even the smallest and seemingly unimportant detail may receive an uncomfortable level of scrutiny. The more elevated a manager is in the organization, the more the level of inspection of details increases. And they will not alert you to this sensitivity. An inappropriate word choice on the part of someone who does not understand the rules gets amplified to a full-on red alert.

Management is really sensitive to people not working together. The gain on this is set to eleven. Anti-social behavior, public displays of refused collaboration, and passive-aggressive actions will be noted. Leave this unconstructive behavior to those who are comfortable being unemployed.

Cultivating a candid relationship with your immediate supervisor is a beautiful thing. You can share whatever when it is just the two of you in private.

Be judicious with your supervisor's boss in meetings or conversations. Frame things in a positive way. Even if others start complaining or making negative statements, do not join in.

In interactions with management senior to your bosses' boss, you should always be a ray of sunshine. *We did great things today, we are doing great things tomorrow, this will be a great year, and next year will be even better.* It is not your job to deliver a message other than positive awesomeness to anyone above your supervisor's level. Following this strategy with senior/executive management also prevents the unfortunate situation where you deliver news not in alignment with your supervisor's last update to their boss. Now the big boss has two conflicting messages. The official one from your supervisor, and another one—likely poorly structured—from a whiny employee.

Good luck with that.

Sales 24/7

My undergraduate education included a class titled "Quality." It had nothing to do with quality in the general sense. It was really a class about what an engineer's real-world career could be like.

The professor had numbered rules. The first was that you are in sales all the time. Every meeting, every call, you are selling what you are trying to accomplish.

I would agree. The world looks at you through the lens of what you write, say, do, and how you look. Each of those is how you sell others on you and what you are trying to achieve. And this all starts with *Credibility*.

It is a worthy goal to polish how you present yourself and your skills of persuasion and emulate sales in your project management activities.

Perception is reality

Perception is reality. This insight was taught to me, and now I pass it to you.

There are videos of people wearing virtual reality goggles and reacting as if what they see is real. Their perception is their reality.

This is true of many beliefs and phenomena project managers will encounter during project execution.

Managing perception is a skill. Do not start with telling people their perception is wrong or not real. Project management is about the practical accomplishment of tasks, not bringing the light of universal truth to the world.

Develop perception sensitivity and the communications filter needed to constructively engage this phenomenon.

Show me the money!

Managers are the leaders and cheerleaders of the organization. They have demonstrated dedication to the organization, culture, and team. For a manager, calmness and staying positive are key. As are skills in strategy, organization, people management, communication, and—especially—political sensitivity.

The management experience is driven by budgets, efficiencies, ROIs, and labor costs. They communicate in money. Approaching with a value proposition is key.

If you are looking to engage management, at a minimum, some part of that discussion must include money. Top-line impact. Bottom-line impact. The financial benefit to the ask.

The, "I feel this" or "Wouldn't this be nice" approaches will fail. Management will be diplomatic in the reply you receive, but this feel/nice approach will accomplish nothing.

You will also have also identified yourself as not-manager material.

If action from management is the goal, show them the money.

Not important, useful

During a planned visit to the European headquarters of my employer, I was going to spend time with the technical support person I work with almost daily. Shortly before making the trip, I had to cancel and reschedule. It was a rude last-minute thing, and I felt an explanation was in order. The CEO's assistant had crushed our meeting, replacing it with one where I met with the CEO.

I took a screenshot of the change and shared it. We rescheduled, and when we finally met, my colleague commented on how I am important to have such a meeting with the CEO, making it out like I was a senior manager or some other higher role in the hierarchy. I immediately clarified the situation. I am not important, I am useful. There is a difference.

Perhaps being useful is the result of the progression of project management skills and experience. At some point in your project manager journey you may find yourself being categorized as "useful."

Useful people are often mistaken for being important. Useful people are often directly tasked by important people with important efforts. Important people are comfortable delegating to useful people. It is not unusual for useful people to wield serious authority and power (temporarily). They also know better than to abuse the situation or let it go to their head. The big stick is only on loan.

Management loves useful people. Those who consistently deliver while requiring minimal maintenance. Management responds to useful like cats respond to catnip.

The good news is, when you're useful, your project efforts will enjoy a high level of support. Useful people work on interesting things and get to accomplish a lot.

The bad news: You will be very busy. Useful people are tasked heavily. The difficulty level will be high. Much of what you will be assigned will have high visibility. You will be specifically selected for tasks that will be genuinely awful—simply because management wants a useful person to execute them.

If you are looking for maximum challenge or an environment that will push your skill development to the limit, learn to be useful.

Project management is not a selfish activity

If there was ever a role requiring servant leadership, project management is it.

Project success should not be just about you. The goal is the execution of the project and the success of the organization and your colleagues.

Supporting your colleagues' and contributors' success is an important part of the project.

A good project manager does not need to cheerlead for themselves. Your excellence will be obvious. Instead, use the goodwill generated from delivering quality results to build up the team. This is an investment of the political capital generated from a successful project outcome that can be reinvested in future success (*Credibility*). This builds a positive, self-reinforcing team.

Share your colleagues' excellence with the leadership. Give credit where credit is due.

When others know being on your team (or your being part of their team) is a positive outcome for all involved, future project execution benefits.

Manager's prerogative

Frogs at the bottom of the well only see part of the sky.
– Chinese proverb

Insight: Management has more information than you do. And they will not be sharing that information with you. This dynamic results in management decisions that at times do not make sense to you. This is how a hierarchical organization works.

The point is, you will find management making decisions that are honestly perplexing. They have their reasons, and your approval will not be sought. More will be accomplished by shrugging and rolling with it than by raising your hand and voicing your objections.

Everyone has a boss. Even the CEO reports to a board of directors. With management comes authority and the power to make changes. This includes changing the direction and focus of the organization's efforts. Projects can be altered. Often without warning or explanation.

Do not take it personally. It is likely someone senior to your managers moved the goalposts. Now your manager has to deal with it. Don't make it difficult. They are probably more frustrated than you are. Support the team and make it happen.

That is what project managers do: Make things happen.

Phenomenal cosmic powers in a little bitty living space

Management comes with responsibility and authority. There is also power associated with management roles. That power is really only available for the manager to express in a limited number of conditions. Using power has its own challenges, and HR does not want lawsuits.

This limited power can be a source of frustration for many managers. They have the tools of power to make decisions and direct action, but unfortunately, those opportunities can be few and far between.

When bringing an opportunity to leadership, present a well-defined ask with a clear, concise, high-value proposition (*Show me the money*). Then place *The Easy Button* (more on this later) in front of them.

The ground will figuratively shake from what happens next.

Management cannot value something they do not understand

Be mindful of how actions you take are being perceived. In a complex work environment, project execution can be open to interpretation. For instance, the order in which tasks are being performed or why some project aspect is being left to languish.

If the optics are less than constructive, perhaps there is an opportunity for pre-emptive clarification and managing of expectations.

Don't let negative perceptions escalate due to a lack of sensitivity and a straightforward explanation.

The immune response to taking instruction

Can you take instruction?

You know, to shut up and do what you're told.

It's a skill to be able to set aside your ego and questions . . . and just follow instructions. This is taught in the military, but it unfortunately is not well understood outside that experience.

People do not like being told what to do. The natural inclination is to ask, "Why?"

There are times when you do not need to know or understand something. A person with more experience will instruct you on the actions to take. Perhaps there is not enough time for the explanation. Or information needed for a complete explanation is confidential. There are also those skills that are learned by doing. Someone tells you to do it, and afterward, you are rewarded with understanding.

Then there are those situations where your understanding of what is being asked will influence your actions. The asker does not want that outcome. The preferred approach, then, is your performance without understanding.

Sometimes your supervisor's patience is running low, and they would appreciate someone just doing what they are told for once without turning it into a science project.

There is a shortage of people who can take instruction. A seasoned manager will recognize and value these few executors.

Project management has opportunities to both give and receive instruction. Understanding your own abilities in this space is important. Sensitivity to others' limitations in taking instruction is equally important. Just because you see the value in this topic does not mean others do.

Acknowledging this phenomenon and developing expertise brings another dimension to your project management efforts.

Management loves surprises!

No, they do not.

With management, surprises are not good. They happen, but you certainly don't want management to be the last to know. Develop the foresight to know when to tell your boss if something's off. The skill of intuitively realizing who needs to know what and when will save you much grief.

A twist on this is the need to communicate information that your supervisor should not take immediate action on. This is not being a snitch or ratting people out. There is information with long-term consequences management may not have visibility to. It takes a judgment call as to whether to share or not.

Managers are adept at recognizing the difference between constructive forward-looking insights and weasels trying to use them to advance a personal agenda. They can differentiate between the passive-aggressive efforts of people "telling" on their colleagues from those giving the manager insight into the broader organization. You have to determine if you have a supervisor who can handle the responsibility.

Taking stock of how you categorize information and developing the skills to mitigate preventable management surprises are worthy goals. Your project management efforts can only improve from this.

Don't blame me

Youth and enthusiasm are always
overcome by old age and treachery.
– David Mamet

This quote is an immutable truth.

Some people document things in an attempt at risk avoidance. The Cover Your Ass (CYA) behavior shows up in requests for written confirmation or "this is a bad idea" statements during a meeting. "We can do this, but I am not the one responsible if it goes wrong."

I used to be concerned about being held accountable for something that went wrong. So, I would point out that it was not my idea and/or it was a bad idea. We should not do this or it should have been done differently. The goal being that if someone is going to be held accountable, the manager involved would at least get some of the blame.

FYI, they won't get any of the blame. If persecution of the innocent is required to deliver a sacrificial lamb, it is just going to happen. And the first choice will be the whiner who has been complaining the whole time that it was a bad idea. And who then tried to make management responsible.

Be positive. Be mindful of how what you do and say looks to management.

Surviving mistakes

Nobody ever thinks about this one ahead of time. Then, when mistakes happen, there is a mad dash to resolve the situation with minimal damage. Mistakes happen, so plan ahead.

Human beings are not accuracy machines. The error rate of humans while engaged in repetitive tasks or when making decisions is disturbingly high. A case could be made that we probably should not be allowed to do these types of things. But, since nothing will get done if humans do not do it, we will just have to make do.

When I worked as a factory mechanic, there was this guy who worked in production. Good attitude, always showed up on time, took instruction well, and worked hard. Two weeks in, he hurt himself drilling something in the drill press. This involved a trip to the emergency room.

A few weeks after that, he cut through the power cord of the saw he was sawing with. Not long after, there was another accident. Perhaps a week later, he was let go. I asked my boss—the person who did the firing—why. He told me the guy is a good employee except he is accident-prone. You can't train that out of someone, and they can't stay in the factory because of it. He had to let him go.

We all have crossed paths with someone whose error rate is so high it forces action.

It should be noted that making mistakes can have an upside. The learning curve from mistakes is steep. There is a reason they call it the school of hard knocks. Screw up enough times (so long as you learn from your mistakes), survive, and remain persistent, and it will pay off eventually. It is a rough path, but the long-term benefit is worth it.

Regardless of your goal to flawlessly deliver a project, you should put some thought into being prepared for mistakes (by you or others) derailing some or all of your project. A little paranoia goes a long way here.

Managers are people too

A moment of self-reflection that may help interactions with management is asking yourself if you are someone you would want to manage. Would you want you as a direct report?

Presented in this chapter were project management phenomena and sensitive topics around interaction with supervisors and management. Tread lightly and think through your engagement when starting your skill development path in this space. Gauge where your management is at on these concepts. Change management opportunities abound here.

Engaging management is a requirement for project management. Take the time to develop expertise maximizing the value of those interactions.

CHAPTER 5

Recurring-Project Phenomena

During the execution of the project, a project manager will likely experience the peculiar phenomena detailed in this chapter. These situations seem to happen when a group of people is working together toward a common goal. Or at least trying to collaborate toward a common goal.

Let's figure this out before the adults get involved

Collective recognition of the path forward does not spontaneously happen. Communication skills are required to align the team. Unfortunately, if that message does not land with a contributor, progress will not occur. And that lack of progress is resistant to the polite, professional efforts of the project manager to get the project back on schedule.

An important skill is recognizing when this type of block to progress is happening.

If management's expectations have been shared and progress is not delivered, there will come a point when leadership will engage and inspect the situation closely. Management is not looking for opportunities to solve simple problems ("simple" is purposefully used here). When they have to get involved and realize the problem is due to one person not working with the rest, the outcome cannot be good. People are not hired to demonstrate incompetence or their inability to work with others.

This "adults get involved" phenomenon requires at least two people for it to occur. If the task in question could be performed by yourself, it would already be complete and there would be nothing to discuss. This means someone is not engaging. Make sure it is not you. The contributor may have good reasons for not engaging. As project manager, you will not.

The approach I practice to mitigate these situations is if after all your communication efforts have failed, share with the team how we should work this out "before the adults get involved." Positive collaboration is important. Advocate for the team performing as needed without management micromanaging.

If, after all this effort, progress remains elusive, then this is probably the time to update your supervisor on the situation (*Management loves surprises!*).

Excellent communication skills are needed to address these situations. Even with acknowledgment and the skills, this phenomenon can be problematic. There are contributors who will refuse to acknowledge the situation and engage responsibly. Thereby forcing the issue to the undesirable management-mediation outcome. My experience is that when a project demonstrates this phenomenon, it is 50/50 that management will need to lean in.

The self-organizing fallacy

There is a commonly held belief that people in small groups self-organize.

No, they do not.

My experience: There are natural leaders who intuitively organize people.

And there are those who have worked with a leader who knows how to organize people and learned from them how it is done.

The remaining balance have no idea how to properly organize, collaborate, and work together as a team.

Taking a group of people, calling them a team, and telling them to organize and make things happen is problematic. And that's regardless of their education, skill, or individual intellect. A well-organized and executing team is a beautiful thing, and they rarely organically occur. This is my experience, though it contradicts the commonly shared corporate propaganda. I am just calling it the way I see it.

The propaganda sets expectations that confuse people when teams are created and given instructions to execute. The participants think they will gel organically and natural self-organization will take over. This creates frustrations when the team dynamics do not meet expectations.

Working effectively as a team is a discipline and learned skill. Experience and maturity improve the collaborative experience.

Exposure to a capable and competent leader will help develop skills in this area. Associate with these people whenever possible. Make yourself useful to them and soak up that leadership goodness.

Participating in, and management of, teams is a skill requirement for project management. Awareness is a goal here. Find a mentor to question. Or find a leader you respect who demonstrates this discipline and follow them as much as you can. Emulation will have some trial-and-error aspects, but valuable experience will be earned from the effort.

The ABCDE incidence – circular prioritization

A not-unusual experience in project management is having priorities change in response to new information. Many organizations have project lists that are reviewed, weighted, prioritized, updated, and altered on a regular basis.

A phenomenon I have seen repeated over and over is described below:

A project execution list is currently in this order: A B C D E

A week later, new information, a customer complaint, new initiative, etc. draws leadership's attention. The priority is rearranged slightly: D A B C E

The teams working on B and C respond to the change by pointing out the importance of their projects. Compromises are made, and the order is updated: B C D A E

The changes to the order alter some of the weighting and priorities and a previously settled fifth-place project has its position upgraded, resulting in another new order of projects: E B C D A

A manager who was on vacation while all of these changes occurred returns, and after a week of digging out, he learns of the priority changes while he was out. A meeting is immediately called to address his concerns. The newly updated project order: A B C D E

Numerous time-consuming meetings, jockeying, emergency evaluations, responses, negotiations, and so many emails later, and the project order ends up back where it was originally. There are variations on this scenario to arriving right back where everyone started, but we have all seen this general scenario unfold.

My observation from witnessing these situations happening over and over again: They are driven by the imperative that leaders be seen taking action. In the above example, multiple actions were taken. Priorities were changed several times. Many expensive hours were wasted. The opportunity cost alone boggles the mind. It is a truly appalling and irresponsible waste of resources.

The goal here is not to promote inflexibility or prevent change. Only to share what is not often acknowledged. Management may have good reason for making priority changes. However, if the priority changes become circular, some explanation may help with morale.

Changing priorities confuse those executing projects and waste resources. Psychologically, it is hard on the team. Consider also the resources conserved and opportunity costs avoided by acknowledging these unconstructive exercises.

The crap/perfection juxtaposition

*The greatest shortcoming of the human race is our
inability to understand the exponential function.*
– Albert Allen Bartlett

As a home project, I tiled the floor in the entryway to my
house. Myself, by my own hand. And not just laying square tile in
neat rows. It involved a diagonal pattern with multiple sizes of
different tiles. And there are three intricate patterns hand
assembled from a variety of specialized tiles. It was ridiculously
difficult, and the amount of time I put into it was beyond the pale.
But it looks awesome. Something you might see in the home of
someone with a much higher net worth than mine.

I did good work, but it is not perfect. I know where all the
flaws are. Including that one imperfection where the four corners
of four tiles do not exactly line up.

This particular story is to show how perfection is not a real
thing. Perfection is a fallacy. An extreme form of thinking often
delivered as a byproduct during the pursuit of excellence.
Achieving the best possible outcome balanced against the efficient
use of resources is a worthy goal. Setting a project's sights on
perfection is a source of eternal frustration and disappointment.
Stop doing it.

"We will have a perfect delivery."

Famous last words. The real-world delivery spectrum ranges
from 100% crap to 100% perfect. At 90% perfection and above,
the project's time and resource requirements begin approaching
infinity.

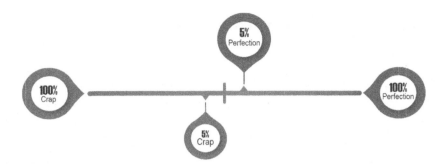

Since projects exist for a reason, typically to deliver value, it is safe to assume non-completion will deliver 100% crap. If the project resolves a known gap, then as long as the project is incomplete, the 100% crap situation is experienced. Only a completed project will deliver value by filling the gap.

A 1% crap delivery is still significantly better than the status quo (100% crap). The resources consumed in delivering 1% crap are significantly lower than 90% perfect. Delivering 1% crap may reduce the pain in a meaningful way (improvement from 100% crap). A 1% crap delivery can be an intermediate goal while the resources are mustered for a 90% perfect solution.

Getting comfortable with a less than 100% perfect delivery saves significant resources. Especially if at the time of defining the project scope not all variables can be properly defined. As long as a less than perfect delivery still delivers useful value of sufficient magnitude to justify the project's expense, it can be considered an acceptable goal.

It is not unusual for a 1% crap delivery to significantly improve the value of a 90% perfect delivery. Things are learned at the 1% crap milestone, and those lessons learned can impact the next sprint to 90% perfect.

An example is a project to deliver a list of ten potential updates. Delivering a list of nine is still very useful. Having an update with the tenth included at a later date is better than making sales wait and wait while that tenth example is hunted down.

A project creating a complete list of the components for an automobile would be an example where 100% perfect is required. No one is interested in a car without wheels.

The fundamental concept is that many, if not most, projects deliver their value in gradients. And these gradients are often non-linear. Good examples are projects that improve on a current situation. Even small, easy to accomplish, incremental efforts deliver meaningful value. These significant gains from small efforts can be drowned out when there is an imperative for perfect outcomes.

Of course, nobody can be faulted for not accepting less than perfection. Which is why some people are hooked on perfect deliveries. No explanations are ever needed with perfect. Perfect requires no compromise. Perfect is easy to demand. Requiring perfect is also another CYA activity. Requiring perfect and accepting nothing less puts the recipient in a risk-free space. Of course, not much of anything constructive gets done, but that is how CYA environments function.

The goal of a project manager is to deliver, not find excuses to support a fetish for risk aversion. Learn how the gradients between 100% crap and 100% perfection in your projects will deliver value. It is the non-linear aspect of those gradients where the real value in project execution is found.

Understanding the *The crap/perfection juxtaposition* concept has the potential to deliver speed, increased value, and decreased costs.

Where the hell are the goal posts going?

At the end of a project, when completion is imminent, a manager gets cold feet. They will perform a panicked inspection. Was anything missed? Is there something we can cram in at the last minute? Will perfection be delivered?

The aspects of the project that connect to them are hastily reviewed and risk aversion kicks into overdrive. Last-minute changes will be hammered into the project. The elegant, on-time delivery just evaporated.

This behavior is classic CYA behavior.

It helps to know in advance that this phenomenon may pop up. Take care in what information is shared just before project completion. This is not a recommendation to mislead or obfuscate. Just be judicious in your language so as to not trigger a management meltdown. Most managers are pleased when a project is delivered. There are a few who are paranoid some detail will come back to haunt them. This can spiral into paralysis by analysis.

Make sure you have other (steadier) people involved in these communications (*Allies*). These should be managers who value more than CYA on minor details. Hopefully they provide guidance and/or run interference, assisting in preventing delivery derailment.

Peeling the onion: An iterative approach

Building on *The crap/perfection juxtaposition* concept is the iterative or "peeling the onion" approach.

This phenomenon can include several different scenarios. When the goal is not well-defined and an approach is difficult to determine. There are times when the path forward is not visible. There are too many undefined variables, or project information is disjointed and unrelated.

Start by writing it all down. In any order. After the info dump, go back through it all. The way to organize the information will reveal itself. This is an iterative process similar to brainstorming.

An experience to share: My supervisor assigned me to update some product brochures. This was at a large corporation operating in the matrix environment. The marketing and communications staff used software accessed on my computer. A draft copy was made available for commenting on the changes.

After my first round of comments, there was a review. I saw obvious opportunities for improvement in the new draft. These were not obvious in the previous draft. I commented again and resubmitted. We went through the edit-and-update process three times. In my humble opinion, the final product was much better the first round's output.

My supervisor scolded me for taking too long. This was to be a one-edit-and-complete task. He had a point. A slam-it-out, single review is quick and completes the task. But how much value can be added with the additional polishing stages? Plus, there is an opportunity cost to the iterative approach. Instead of working on a second or third round of edits, you could be delivering value in another task.

The time commitment for a second, or third, review is typically much less than the first. Relative to the value delivered, iterations two and three likely have a very high return on investment. Those customer-facing brochures I thoroughly edited will benefit the company exponentially for years to come through an improved customer experience.

During the early stages of a project, these iterative reviews deliver significant value. Taking into account what is revealed after the initial establishment of the project and feeding that back into the next round of planning will deliver a positive non-linear ROI as the project progresses.

My experience is that the value is not in the first pass. The second or third pass is when peak value is delivered. After the third pass, it is likely diminishing returns. Infinite iteration does not deliver infinite value. Infinite iteration is a fallacy aligning with the CYA pursuit of perfection concept. An eyes-open approach to the real value delivered by each round of iteration prevents over analysis from happening.

Email writing benefits from the iterative approach. Write that first draft and go back through with a re-read. You will find word-choice and sentence-structure improvements. Spelling errors, duplications, extra words, etc. That second pass delivers significant value in improving the success of the communication. For those critical, leadership, or customer-facing communications, a third pass is not a bad idea. There are situations where having a colleague read the draft email may even be warranted.

Some projects are not well understood during the beginning stages. The desired final outcome is clearly understood, but the path from start to completion is unknown. In many ways, this is like a writer starting a new book and staring at that blank page. Time and energy will be inefficiently applied trying to find that perfect path on day one.

My writing goal has never been to get it correct the first time. I put something down, accept its imperfections, and go to work improving it. If you were to review this book's manuscript as it developed over a year's time, you would be shocked at the incoherency of the message at times. Everything was initially written as a raw concept and then worked, re-worked, and polished into its current state through an iterative process.

Many authors will share how many times they had to re-write a novel before it could be published. There are similar parallels in project management. When planning a project, after establishing the path to completion, alternatives reveal themselves. Until the process of planning happens, the options for improved efficiency are not revealed. Each pass through the planning process continuously improves the outcome.

Management is not all that comfortable with an iterative approach. They are more aligned with a single-effort-and-done approach. The *Making the sausage* and the *Peeling the onion* approaches have synergies. A developed skill in leveraging the *Making the sausage* concept can be integrated as part of the *Peeling the onion* approach. The energy and time savings from *Making the sausage* more than make up for the time lost to a second and third iteration. The final positive non-linear ROI delivered supports developing this skill combination.

Peeling the onion is an expert concept because of the subtleties to how many iterations you need, what should be iterated, and what is included in each iteration. If this process is new to you, take it in small steps.

Introducing the *Peeling the onion* to your project management efforts may require elements of change and expectation management. Your colleagues and management are not going to understand what you are doing. Be mindful of this, and gently work on raising awareness. Going headfirst into *Peeling the onion* can be problematic without buy-in from your supervisor.

The non-linear improvements in value, quality, and innovation *Peeling the onion* brings to project management efforts make it worth the time and effort.

Technical correctness

When a technical product fails to deliver, the baleful glare of management will fall on those involved like the Hammer of Doom. This is something that is just understood, whether the issue is not performing as advertised, premature failure, or an epic crash and burn.

The fear of this happening drives behavior that complicates the project management effort. Contributors are highly motivated to make sure the product performs absolutely flawlessly. The goal of perfect delivery rears its ugly head once again.

"Absolutely" is like that word "perfection." Achieving 100% absolute surety comes with costs approaching infinity. You can hedge risk, but you cannot ever be 100% sure.

Engineers are typically perfectionists—to a degree greater than the average population. The same applies to their OCD (obsessive compulsive disorder) behavior. Both of these demonstrated personality traits are important to the success of the engineer's efforts. It is important to understand this upfront when engaging engineers as project managers. Thus, both by personality and by profession, perfection appeals to engineers. Watch for it. Plan for it.

Combining an engineer's risk-averse nature and perfectionist leanings with a technical subject bring you to "correct implementation."

There is a correct way to accomplish what is being asked. An engineer will state this with absolute, perfect surety. Other implementations would work but are less than ideal. Ideal solutions often present commercial challenges. Correct implementation is almost always impossible due to cost and time limitations. A project's technical discussion must stay away from ideal or perfect solutions. Instead, anchor the development efforts in best practices, existing proven tech, or solutions built from previous experience. A well-defined specification will make a significant difference. The more ambiguity, the more engineers veer toward ideal solutions and correct implementation.

Remember, engineers have an ideal design itch they wish to scratch. If a window of opportunity is presented, they will move the approach to ideal. Be prepared ahead of time, ask lots of questions, and keep this concept in mind.

There is a difference between what is ideal and what is practically possible. In many ways, this a variant of *The crap/perfection juxtaposition.*

It should be noted that there is nothing wrong with an engineer's leaning toward correct implementation. This pursuit of excellence and adherence to acknowledging real-world impact is important to engineering success. The point of acknowledging this phenomenon is to curb the more extreme fetish aspects when project management is executing a practical delivery.

Hooking on

Just as your project is getting off the ground, have you ever been approached by someone in the organization with this comment? "I heard your project is moving forward. That's great. We have been needing this to happen for a long time. You know what would also be great? Adding XYZ to your project. It is not a big ask."

A project is chartered and organized. The team is on board and execution begins. When the project begins moving forward, someone will point out how this project lends itself to another goal. The argument presented is that while the project executes, completing some other related tasks would be easy enough to do.

This is *Hooking on*. The tactic of using a project and project manager's time and energy to accomplish other tangential tasks without contributing resources to the main effort. It gives the project manager all the extra work and complexity with no increase in final delivered value.

Hooking on is the project front-end cousin to the back-end *Where the Hell are the goal posts going?*. *Hooking on* is not the risk-panic event that is *Where the Hell are the goal posts going?*, but it is an attempt to cram something into a project while adding little to no value to the core effort.

Catching others trying to attach their work to an already scoped and chartered project is obvious once you know what to look for.

Hooking on is also a version of scope creep. "You're updating those documents? That's great! This has needed to be done for a long time. Did you include these others? It would be good if they all get done at the same time." Management may also see a project moving forward and attach additional deliverables. The siren call of hooking onto a project in motion is difficult to resist for many people frustrated with the inefficiencies of a matrix organization.

Hooking on can spiral out of control and completely change a project into something that no longer works. Whoever is making the request is taking advantage of the situation for their benefit at the project's expense. This can derail a project as the *Hooking on* requirements begin to expand. It is important for a project manager be sensitive to this possibility and guard against it.

What just happened?

I am as constant as the northern star.
– Julius Caeser

What has been seen cannot be unseen
–   C.A. Wolf

And it's going to happen again, and again. It has to happen.
It's not what I want. But what I want doesn't matter.

– Dexter

Having read this chapter there is no going back. What has been learned here cannot be unlearned. Were the reader to work on projects from now until the sun grows cold and dark, they will never escape the recurrence of this chapter's phenomena.

Every project manifest's one or more of the phenomena in this chapter, over and over again. Just like *Ground Hog Day*.

And now you will recognize when it happens.

Enjoy.

CHAPTER 6

The Dark Side of Communications

A salesperson is visiting a customer. The customer relates a technical challenge. The salesperson replies they do not have the answer but will bring the engineer along at the next visit in two weeks. The customer's need is not immediate, and they agree to wait until the next visit.

Two weeks later, the salesperson and subject-matter-expert engineer sit down with the customer.

The customer tells them about the application, their approach, and the unproductive outcome.

The engineer looks at the customer and asks, "Why are you doing it like that? That's stupid."

This is an extreme example of communication gone bad. But there are situations, communication styles, and sometimes just people, delivering outcomes not all that different from this story.

Communications can secure success as well as deliver failure. You should be aware of the negative communication phenomena that happen too often in project management. Effectively identifying and navigating bad communication skills is equally important to developing good communication skills.

Unleash the fury!

Let's take a moment to discuss frustration.

What a topic! If frustration could be bottled and used to generate energy, project management could power the world. The sources of frustration are many and never-ending: misunderstandings, last-minute changes, management charging in at inconvenient times and smashing everything, etc. Fun times.

In the professional work environment, frustration is a real and ongoing challenge that impacts mental health and generates strong negative emotions. Frustration is the response to unreasonable and stupid situations. If people are involved, then frustration happens.

If you are not an emotionless robot, experiencing frustration will be an ongoing condition while managing projects. **Have you ever evaluated your frustration response?**

Identifying those frustrating situations, acknowledging them, and then having a plan will help manage your response. It starts with realizing frustration is real and will recur. Then you must self-evaluate and take stock of where you're at with this phenomenon. If you struggle with self-reflection or just want an extra perspective, a mentor can be helpful. Once you have an idea where your current frustration responses are at, the next steps are fairly obvious.

My own experience with developing a constructive frustration response was a long-term challenge. When I was a little boy, my mother told me I am part Irish and part German, meaning I will get angry quickly and stay angry forever. She was not wrong. Frustration leads to anger, and this leads to likely saying or writing things I will regret.

The evaluation process is not about ignoring frustration. The emotional response is delivering important information. Use it. The goal is to have a response that does not damage long-term relationships or add more problems to your project efforts.

Learn to stay frosty and engaged. Work through the challenge. I've learned that these situations are opportunities to demonstrate skill in resolving a difficult situation. Show leadership and provide guidance.

Frustration is often the result of poor communication. Developing your communication skills will reduce the number of frustration events you have. A little empathy can help also. The source of the frustration may be getting slammed with work. Or they are dealing with unreasonable requests. Or maybe a project manager is not asking the right questions. Perhaps some assistance and guidance from you or someone else will get the whole thing back on track.

Frustration and email (or any kind of instant messaging) are a toxic combination. Before you respond while you're frustrated, get up and walk away. The desire to unleash the fury will be strong. If you don't take a breather before responding, you might just write a career-limiting email. Remember, emails are forever.

Whatever you do, do not give in to the frustration and make sarcastic remarks, yell, or insinuate. Of all the phenomena presented in this book, keeping your frustrated reactions under control could be the most challenging skill to develop.

Setting the world on fire

You cannot control the world, but you can set the tone and influence the outcome of many of your own situations.

We live in a world where people are often unaware of their word choices or context. They have a sense of entitlement to say what they wish. Or even worse, what they feel. And they do this in any setting, personal or professional.

For your part, do not say anything inflammatory. It is that simple. "Simple" itself can be an inflammatory word, but in this case, it perfectly captures the absolute nature of this approach. Avoiding inflammatory statements, both written and verbal, will feel like an IQ test at times. Because it is. Figuring out what and when something is inflammatory is a skill to be developed. There is a contextual dynamic to this approach depending on the who, where, and why.

In addition to your own journey to remain constructive and avoid the inflammatory, you will likely need to lessen any inflammatory communications that flow through you. Then you can help others better understand the impact of ill-thought-out and delivered communications.

Insinuation and gossip are verboten

Don't insinuate or gossip. It is unprofessional.

To determine if discussing a topic with a colleague is gossip, I ask myself: Will sharing this benefit the company? If not, it is probably gossip.

The free-association apocalypse

During a project's planning stage, there is no cost in adding to its scope, so other people involved will keep expanding it. This means your deliverable will keep getting harder—and likely impossible—to reach.

This is a tough situation to resolve, especially if management is engaging in this behavior. No pre-determined, easy-to-use, silver-bullet solution exists.

The best you can do is keep redirecting back to the projects original scope. Ask detailed questions probing the offending request for expansion. Hopefully someone on your team recognizes free association when they see it and can help keep the creativity focused on practical innovation versus wish-listing.

Having read this, you will most likely recognize *The free-association apocalypse* the next time it happens. You may even be remembering when this last happened right now.

Maximum talking, minimum content

Conversations or meetings should be like a game of tennis. You speak, answer a question, or make a point. Then another person speaks, answers a question, or makes a point. The conversation goes back and forth. Everyone participates as needed and limits the discussion to the agreed topics while giving each participant the opportunity to speak.

The "how" of conducting oneself in a conversation is not universally understood. We have all been in meetings with someone who just cannot stop talking, and talking, and talking.

Judging the level of appropriate sharing in the conversation is a sign of maturity. If you find yourself talking for more than twice as long as the other speaker(s), you should probably rein it in.

As we covered in *Forty-Three seconds,* keep to the facts and nothing but the facts. Say what needs to be said, then shut up.

However, there will be meetings where a *Maximum talking, minimum content* takes over the conversation. Learn how to break in and redirect. You may have to start talking over them and keep talking until they stop. Then redirect. Don't make it personal or bring attention to their domination of the conversation. Just redirect, doing the minimum to keep the conversation on track.

If the *Maximum talking, minimum content* is a repeat offender and you are challenged in keeping the conversation on course, try forming an alliance with another participant. Between the two of you, maneuver the conversation where it needs to be.

Over the course of your project management career, there will be many meetings and many *Maximum talking, minimum content* experiences. Learn how to identify them and guide the discussion back to something all the participants can engage in.

Unnatural conversation

To set the scene: The team is gathered around a conference room table. Topics are listed on a whiteboard. Perhaps a presentation is on the big screen. There is a lively discussion ongoing. People are taking turns to speak their piece.

Then a topic comes up that one participant latches onto. And they keep talking about it. Expounding and elaborating, drilling down to a level of minutia far outside the scope of this meeting.

And then someone else jumps on the bandwagon. A whirlwind of nostalgia, technical detail, and dreams of things for the future continues on. *Maximum talking, minimum content* manifests as a group phenomenon. Then the meeting runs out of time, ending as a gigantic waste of time.

You have just participated in a session of *Unnatural conversation*. Someone was bored and feeling unstimulated. When they were able to get hold of the conversation, they steered it to a tangentially related topic, and then spoke at length about something they find more interesting. Others joined in. No one stopped the process and much time was wasted.

There is a subtle difference between this and *The free-association apocalypse*. *Unnatural conversation* is several participants talking ad nauseum about unrelated topics to a tiny level of detail. *The free-association apocalypse* is the seemingly never-ending addition of complexity to a project without concern for practicality.

Unnatural conversation is an unconstructive and undisciplined use of time. If the person starting it is more senior, you might have to grin and bear it. In other situations, anticipate and strategize how you will get the conversation back under control. You will find certain individuals are more susceptible than others to engaging in this kind of behavior.

Aside from regaining control during the meeting, perhaps schedule shorter meetings where the time pressure makes *Unnatural conversation* difficult. Making others aware of this phenomenon can also help.

This phenomenon is another where awareness is the biggest part of solving the problem. Once acknowledged, you will recognize it almost instantly.

Can God create a rock bigger than God can lift?

In project management, this concept manifests in two ways. It could be either the derailing of a meeting with needless speculation, or a request for something so far out of the ordinary it is difficult to respond. It seems to me that this happens when either someone is trying to impress you with how smart they are, or the requesting party does not understand the practical limitations of the subject being discussed. Perhaps there is a third possibility: They are just trying to see what you will deliver in response. A test of sorts. For the purpose of this discussion, only the first two will be addressed.

Take the example of a meeting or conversation, often technical in nature, when the line of discussion deviates to tangentially relevant topics. You receive questions or comments delivering little to no value to the meeting topic, or the questions require a ridiculous amount of work to answer while providing little in return. This often happens as part of *Maximum talking, minimum content* scenario.

Otherwise, this comes up in customer-facing engagements. Someone asks, "What if the application was upside down, at 10,000 meters above sea level, there are traces of chlorine in the air, and the operator speaks Icelandic. How would your product perform?"

This is so far out of ordinary operation, there is no way to answer it. To test or determine a detailed response is not worth the effort. They are essentially asking if God can create a rock bigger than God can lift. The question serves no practical purpose.

In sales-related situations, however, saying no is not an option. Just because something has never been tested does not mean it will not work. But do you want your name associated with giving permission to a very non-standard application?

If you do not have an answer to the question, *Never make it up*.

My response to such bizarre questions is to add "speculate" to the beginning of my reply. It's my favorite "get out of jail free" word. Rather than saying "no" or "that is not an appropriate use of the product" (which are both negative statements), I say something like, "That has not been tested and performance is not guaranteed, but based on past performance, I speculate the outcome could be X." It answers the question without committing to it.

Some may argue this answer dodges a specific answer to the question and therefore lacks integrity and will negatively impact credibility. I disagree. The question was hardly airtight and complete in its structure. Much is left unsaid, and the person asking the question is reserving the right to take a precise answer and apply it to an imprecise situation. And if the final outcome is not perfect, they WILL call you on it.

With words like "speculation" and "possible but not tested," the discussion can remain engaged without delivering a commitment.

Ultimately, cases of the *Can God Create a Rock Bigger Than God Can Lift* phenomenon are a smart person scratching a mental itch or injecting extreme risk avoidance. My experience is they do not plan to implement their unlikely scenario. By "speculating" but not "guaranteeing," you give them a safe answer without committing to anything. A response has been delivered, satisfying whatever motivated the question in the first place. The "speculate" wording also pushes the liability back on the person who asked the question. Allowing the requestors individual risk aversion to resolve the situation without need for further discussion...

Parallel communications

This is my favorite communication challenge. It's common but also the least understood. A phenomenon as rampant as it is costly.

As an application engineer, you will have direct access to customers; inside access right to the key decision makers. This situation—left brain–centric engineers communicating directly with the customer—is a sensitive issue for sales managers. The sales manager may have invested years, if not decades, developing trust and credibility with the customer, and now those customers will be speaking directly to a left-brained source of information with an underdeveloped customer-facing communications filter. What could go wrong?

This all goes wrong when communications are not inclusive. To avoid problems, always copy the sales manager on any email exchanges. Invite the sales manager to meetings, etc.

Otherwise, parallel communication streams develop. Problems are shared and resolved without key stakeholders being in the know. Different groups communicate and engage on the same topic while being ignorant of each other's efforts.

The true sin here is not the confusion and negative communications experience; it's opportunity cost. Parallel communication wastes people's time.

A variant of parallel communication is called shotgunning. This is when someone is looking for information and so shoots off a bunch of emails, instant messages, and calls to several key people. All this in looking for a single piece of information. This drives a hellishly expensive consumption of resources while several people look for a single answer. The opportunity cost of shotgunning boggles the mind. Stop doing it.

What to do? Most individuals engaging in parallel communication and shotgunning do not even realize they are doing it. Gently raise the visibility of these phenomena. Most people will see the problem and self-correct. A select few may require more overt guidance. For the most part, those who are enlightened on this topic get with the program by reducing or eliminating these phenomena from their professional communications experience.

The circular firing squad

Maximum talking, minimum content, Unnatural conversation, and an email make a baby.

Who has not sent an email asking a question only to receive a question in return? You reply with your question clarified and re-send. The next email back is a reply about a subject tangential to the discussion. Another party copied in then replies they heard another group is doing something similar, but not actually the same thing. Another participant in the communication shares this could be done better using this thing not currently part of the product, but if we ever develop it, the results would be awesome.

These are those weird never-ending email strings where no one answers anything and nothing is accomplished. Questions are answered with questions and/or speculation about how something *could* be accomplished. In some cases, participating members digress into topics they are more interested in.

My guess is what's actually happening is everyone involved is really busy and they are skimming the email and not truly engaging in what is being discussed. A rapid response is made to get this one thing done and out of their inbox, with no real mental energy invested.

Learn to recognize these colossal time wasters and have a strategy ready to get them under control.

My solution? Get people on the phone or face-to-face (*In person for maximum effect*). This allows for a more solid engagement and delivers results faster. Sometimes you just have to talk to people.

The meeting sinkhole

In Milwaukee, you can visit the Pabst mansion. The office of the founder of Pabst Brewing Company is there. In that room is only a desk. There are no chairs for anyone other than Mr. Pabst. His policy was you came in, said what needed to be said, and got out. An efficient approach to meetings.

Project managers will organize and participate in many, many meetings. Executing a well-organized meeting delivering constructive outcomes is a beautiful thing. Skill development in meetings benefits from communication skill development. Meetings are a continuous improvement opportunity for everyone. Expertise in this space is more a journey than a destination.

Meetings are a whole subject in themselves, and many, many books have been written how to conduct them properly. Shared below are project management relevant insights into this broad topic.

Meetings serve a limited number of purposes: presentation of information, solicitation of information (asking questions), and seeking consensus (making a decision). In most cases, a meeting is likely a combination of these three basic meeting building blocks.

Meetings should not just "happen". They should serve a pre-planned purpose. Have a plan, and actively manage the progression of the meeting. Be proactive and mindful of what the meeting was called to accomplish. Make absolutely sure the purpose of the meeting is delivered before the end.

Be ready to get the meeting back on track should a participant go off on a tangent.

A trick I have found to keep everyone focused is to shorten the meeting time. Instead of one-hour meetings, try forty-five-minute meetings. Or better yet, thirty-minute meetings. A shorter meeting keeps the participants focused on the reason the meeting is called and reduces the likelihood of meandering discussions.

An aspect of meetings rarely discussed is the cost. Calling a meeting involves real costs, such as the wages and benefits of the attendees and the opportunity cost of their time. What other value could they deliver if everyone was not sitting in the meeting?

Picture a mechanical odometer in a car. The older style with the spinning cylinders. But instead of miles, the numbers represent dollars. The moment the participants arrive at the meeting, the numbers start spinning, adding up the incremental cost, minute by minute. This is the increasing dollar cost of the meeting. The higher the skill level per person, plus an increasing meeting headcount, and that cost counter's rate of increase evolves into a blur.

Acknowledging the value of meetings, having a plan to arrive at the purpose of the meeting, and having the experience to keep them on track will develop your meetings into a machine for accomplishment. A value outcome justifying the cost.

But they are yelling at me

Sometimes people yell. Perhaps not as much in today's work environment, but I have worked in male-dominated, old-school industries where old-fashioned ass-chewing is still practiced.

Handling these unprofessional situations and personalities is part of the project manager experience.

What to do? Regardless of whether you deserve the yelling? Not everyone has the U.S. Army basic training experience with being berated to fall back on. What follows is the guidance I can share.

Stay calm. Do not get angry back. Seriously, learn your natural response to these situations and develop a staying-cool response. This is a difficult skill to master. Especially if the yeller is a top-of-the-line jackass. But stay calm. Listen to their words. Likely, they are yelling because their boss yelled at them or the situation is just too frustrating. Let them get whatever is bothering them out of their system.

Then calmly address their concerns.

Here is the weird part. By not starting a fight in response to their venting, you will actually become closer. After not reacting to the histrionics and remaining professional, this somehow builds your credibility and demonstrates you are a good-faith partner who will stick with them no matter what.

The first time you try this, it will likely take a leap of faith. If you are able to make it through, my guess is what happens on the other side will surprise you.

Sarcasm

Leave the sarcasm at home. Don't do it.

So much about sarcasm is cultural, situational, and tone-dependent. There are those who consider sarcasm great fun and others who will take instant offense.

To be honest, I am a sarcastic person. There is a term ... "sarcotic." It's sarcasm so vicious people can't tell if what you are saying is sarcasm or if you are psychotic. That's where I land with this form of communication.

I have had experiences where colleagues learn about my sarcastic sense of humor and how I am holding back. They would say, "I'm sarcastic too; this will be fun." It was fun for a little while. Then they found out what happens when the Godzilla of sarcasm shows up to play. And this is an example of why you should keep extreme personality traits to yourself.

Many cultures do not support sarcastic interaction. This is my opinion based on my experiences. I worked for a Swiss company with many French and French-Swiss colleagues. Sarcasm is not in their makeup. Perhaps it was an English-as-a-second-language thing, but anything I said was interpreted literally. "Erik, why would you say such a terrible thing?"

My next employer was German. While in Germany for training, one of my colleagues shared that she is very sarcastic and would like to apologize in advance. She shared how she had to be careful because her comments, while hilarious to some people, could be taken as an insult. We had so much fun together. Thank God Germans have a sense of humor.

The point of these examples is to remind you to be cautious with sarcasm. The default should always be to keep the communication professional. You never know who is listening and how they'll interpret what you've said.

We will not be talking about sex

There are subjects that should not be discussed in a professional work environment. Even in casual conversation with colleagues. Similar perhaps to sarcasm, there are things best left unshared.

During a dinner after a global sales meeting in France, a colleague from China tried to engage me, the American, in a discussion around politics.

My reply: "I do not discuss politics, religion, or sex in the work environment." My Chinese colleague was visibly disappointed.

A French colleague leaned across the table and said, "Erik, we are in France. You can talk about sex."

Too funny.

And no, we will not.

Outside the United States, the rules can be very different, but these topics have no place in a professional project management environment.

People being people

Emphasized early in this book is the critical nature of communication proficiency to project management. Familiarity with the strange, less-than-positive communication experiences that manifest in the project management environment is part of the learning experience. Many are addressed by not engaging in them. Others require pro-active effort to manage. A few are personal, representing an opportunity for self-improvement.

Mostly this chapter is about people being people and how to prevent unconstructive communication styles from impacting project execution.

CHAPTER 7

Behavior Phenomena

There are project management phenomena intricately linked to the inner psychology, personality, and life experiences of the people involved. This chapter shares topics about people that likely cannot be changed. The only approaches are engagement and work-arounds; acknowledgment and compensating strategies.

In the case of unconstructive behavior, there is an opportunity to develop people-management skills.

Liability, the project killer

It is easier to ask for forgiveness than permission.
– U.S. Navy Rear Admiral Grace Hopper

Liability can be a contributor-participation killer. High perceived liability can trigger risk-avoidance behavior, complicating project participation. No one wants to be persecuted for negatively impacting a project.

Contributors to projects are mindful of the liability risk associated with a task. This thought of potential negative outcomes influences their enthusiasm. There are those who play it very safe and only move forward with a sure thing. On the other side of the spectrum are the foolhardy. Unique to each contributor, risks and rewards calculated based on project topic interest and personal risk threshold. Most contributors never verbalize this mostly subconscious process.

Risk aversion can drive bizarre behaviors that are less than constructive.

Risk aversion can be identified by the use of everyone's favorite risk-avoidance word: No.

There is nothing fundamentally wrong with saying no. It is good to have people in the organization who can deliver this word. If engineers do not say no, all kinds of bad things happen. No is the word used to prevent bad choices and undesirable outcomes. Without no, bridges fall down, planes fall out of the sky, and condoms fail prematurely. These are just a few examples of what happens when an engineer does not say no when appropriate.

Using "no" to drive the risk to zero is not an appropriate use of this otherwise useful word.

Now, what are some signs of liability concerns? Contributors exhibiting extreme communication behavior.

There are times when no one will say what the problem is. Instead, there will be a continuous re-inspection of project details. Questions answered with questions (*The circular firing squad*). Sometimes it's including a large number of people in every meeting invite or copied in every email. Maybe it's continuously requesting management input or being really evasive in every interaction.

Another method is avoiding delivering a conclusion or assigning responsibility. Some people will keep bringing up details and related topics while avoiding defining a path forward. Each of these manifestations of risk avoidance could be described as the opposite of decisive.

If decisiveness and conclusions remain elusive, risk aversion may be the reason.

You will be on your own figuring this out. Just asking does not work. Honestly, most people do not even know why they are reacting the way they are. It could be subconscious-driven behavior.

Mitigating project contributors' perceived risk is a skill. Yes, perceived. The risk may or may not be real. Its existence is not relevant to the contributor. Their perception is what must be addressed.

The tactics I use most often to get past the risk-aversion shenanigans are transparency and transference. Acknowledge the concerns. Share your understanding. Don't point fingers or try to shame them. This is an opportunity to show leadership and advocate a constructive path forward.

After identifying and publicly sharing the challenge, the quickest way to get things back on track is to transfer the risk to the project manager. Put it in writing or accept it verbally. I, Erik Lange, am requesting this action and fully understand your concerns. Regardless, we are doing this anyway. May God have mercy on our souls.

Your approach will be less melodramatic, but the fundamental goal is to take away their responsibility for the risk. If something goes wrong, it is not their problem. Remember, this is about their perceived risk. In many cases, the project manager is accepting liability for a risk that does not exist.

Contributor participation secured at zero cost. Infinite ROI achieved!

Mitigating risk can have dramatic results. It can transform foot dragging and delay tactics into full-blown enthusiasm. The contributor wants to participate and do the work. They just do not want to be liable if something turns out less than ideal. You may need broad shoulders and possibly asbestos underwear to pull this off. It's definitely not an approach for a novice.

A long-term benefit of risk mitigation is the positive effect it will have on your credibility and the willingness of others to work on your projects. They know an experienced, steady hand is guiding the project. There will be no scapegoating or persecution of the innocent. There is power in this.

Mastery of managing project liability can make the impossible possible. Successfully engaging this phenomenon requires excellent planning and communication skills as well as a well-developed ability to gauge risk. Incorrect execution can have grave consequences.

Left brain versus right brain

One side of the brain is focused on math, reasoning, problem-solving, and logic. The other side is where communication, art, and similar reside. Individuals typically have a dominant side. Engineers lean toward the math and logic side. Salespeople live on the other side. These two sentences explain so much ...

This phenomenon unconstructively manifests with people who spend much of their efforts on the logical side. The result is they are often quite weak in the communications area. Having great ideas and being unable to share them constructively is a challenge to overcome.

My personal experience is that if I am deep into a technical problem, troubleshooting and really pushing, my communication skills suffer. I can see it in the emails I write and the words I use when speaking.

Acknowledgement of this phenomenon goes a long way toward navigating this human limitation. You will have to be patient with people engaged in left-brain activities. They need support in communicating what they are doing.

Although my understanding is each individual has an inherent predisposition to one side or the other, there is the possibility for growth. Left-brain-dominant individuals can work on those communication skills just as right-brain-dominant folks can work on numbers, etc. Even small, incremental improvement delivers real value to your project management efforts.

The quid pro quo discombobulation

What can you do for me? It is a fair request. Why should a contributor in a matrix organization do anything to support this project's requested activities?

There are those who believe that unless you can do something for them there is no motivation to participate. It is logical, after all. If you go to the store to purchase a candy bar, you give the store money in exchange. Should not the same be true for the contributor's valuable time? You require their input to your project, so what are you going to do for them?

The answer is nothing. You will do nothing for them. At least not in the context they are requiring.

Their argument is void in a corporate matrix environment. The employer has already compensated them for their efforts while allowing for flexibility in task execution. This is not an opportunity for third-world-style corrupt shakedowns.

The leadership will set the priorities for project execution. Failure to deliver can be handled by them.

The solution? Keep things polite and professional. Stay engaged with the individual. Document and communicate. Regularly update your leadership. Not to rat out the problem. Nobody likes a snitch. If the contributor's inaction eventually results in delays, it will fall on them to explain.

Insufficient gravitas

It starts like this: Your supervisor assigns you a project. It may be a straightforward, short-timeframe deliverable. Find something out, update a document, and make a presentation.

The person you need to work with has been with the company a long time. You are polite and professional. The ask is well-defined and straightforward. The time required to complete is short.

But they are not responsive. You send out an email. No reply. You set up a meeting. They decline. You call them on the phone and instant message them. Engagement remains elusive.

No matter what you do, there seems to be no way to get the person on board.

Stay professional. Then engage your leadership. There are legitimate times, after all other approaches are exhausted, when asking for support is reasonable. But this only works if you are calm, professional, have documented the lack of engagement, and have a clearly defined ask.

Sometimes the engagement is just copying your boss, or their supervisor, in the email or a cc to a meeting. Or inviting more senior people to a meeting. If this happens often enough, management will figure it out.

Be patient, be professional, never insinuate, and advocate for a positive outcome.

They are a peach

You will meet individuals who are of exceptional abrasiveness. Grumpy, a little angry, blunt, and plain-speaking, they are often inflammatory in their approach to communication.

My experience with such individuals is they are also typically competent and make good project contributors. Their abrasiveness will tone down over time after the initial introduction. You just need a thick skin and to not react to their social impropriety.

Then there are those who complain incessantly to get what they want. Why? Because it works. Like going *Full Kamikaze*, as shared in a later chapter, this is a form of bullying. Complaining is annoying, and most people will give the complainer what they want just to make the complaining stop.

There is a rare version of the peach phenomenon that I call "the rotten peach." A peach taking every interaction to maximum unpleasantness. These negative experiences are likely an indication of a bigger problem.

A rotten peach uses unfriendliness to cover incompetence, driving people away to prevent visibility of poorly delivered outcomes The rotten-peach persona is a survival skill, though this is not a 100% rule. Some people are just assholes. But experience this phenomenon a few times and do a deeper analysis and it will make sense.

Name droppers

Name droppers are a special breed of challenging to work with. They see themselves as very important, and as important people, they only work with important people. They like to drop names during meetings. Often as a way to intimidate or influence.

It gets a little ridiculous at times as the names dropped go up higher and higher in the organization.

What to do? Ignore their unconstructive behavior. The people represented by the dropped names are not likely to have any exposure to the project. If it makes a project contributor feel better to name drop, good for them. It will have no effect on actions taken, though.

Prima donnas

There are those within an organization that have a fairly high opinion of themselves. They are not humble. Perhaps they are high performers or long-term deliverers of value to the company.

Or they may just be arrogant jerks.

As long as the arrogance does not interfere with the project, there is no reason to interfere with their fantasy.

The good news is people exhibiting these behaviors typically lack the depth and humility to develop real skills and therefore are not likely to be needed as project contributors.

Project managers interact with many different personalities. There are some that will not appeal to you. A few may be genuinely offensive.

As long as they deliver and do not adversely affect other contributors on the project, accept their eccentricities. You will work with many people you do not like over the length of your career. Look past the personality and focus on the project.

What did I just read?

Unfortunately, there are some few whose psychology, personality, and social approach present a unique challenge to effective engagement. This chapter presented a number of phenomena where the experience engaging a project contributor requires keeping your focus on the long-term achievement. Not on the short-term irritation. It's likely you have experienced some or even all of them. Just remember that you are not alone in thinking they are difficult to deal with.

CHAPTER 8
Project Execution

How many pre-project meetings have you participated in where everything everyone can think of goes on the whiteboard? Brainstorming gives the project its first baby steps. Perhaps the chicken scratch on the board more resembles the tag cloud of a website than the genesis of an organized project. This is what beginnings often look like: messy.

How to start? What does organized look like? How to make sense of any of this? There is so much to do.

Stay calm and accept the challenge. Large and/or complex projects are difficult by their very nature. Experience will certainly help, but we all must start somewhere. Retain calm professionalism at all times. If you are unsettled, others involved will pick up on that.

There are tools and educational opportunities providing guidance on project organization. Personally, I am a big fan of SaFe Agile. Breaking projects up into short duration efforts helps with individual event-horizon challenges and allows for developmental flexibility as the project situation evolves over time (*Peeling the onion*). It also addresses the challenge that the longer a project is "open," the more likely it will get changed (*Manager's prerogative*).

To be honest, a little OCD also helps with project organization. As long as you can handle the anxiety when progress is challenged. If you are not gifted with OCD, then this may be a skill-development opportunity.

Many projects have an obvious path forward. Some do not. For those with a more complex and nebulous structure, there is an approach I call "the object under a cloth." Picture an object on a tabletop, with its shape and physical details covered by a thin, opaque cloth. It is not possible to determine what the object is because the cloth smooths over its physical details and we cannot just remove the cloth.

The object under the cloth represents the project. The goal is to define the project.

What to do? The next step is *Asking good questions* to gather information about the project. I liken this to driving spikes through the cloth around the perimeter of the hidden object. Each spike pulls the cloth tight, revealing more detail. Skilled execution of this process eventually reveals the shape of the project from underneath the tightly pulled cloth.

What follows in this chapter are the observed phenomena and useful approaches to improving project execution.

In the beginning

Beginnings are always difficult. There are the two beginnings to plan for in your project management experience. Starting out in project management is the first, and it comes with a steep learning curve. The other is beginning a new project and its own unique challenges. Both beginnings benefit from having a plan ahead of time.

Hopefully, when you are new to project management, you can start small. Completing projects with an ever-increasing level of complexity and duration builds confidence. This is the best way for new people to start out. They get built up.

Or you might get thrown into the deep end of the pool.

The beginning of a project can be a considered, planned affair. Development of a roadmap from a defined scope. The scope leading to source and contributor requirements being identified and assigned. This leads to the critical path. Project execution begins when funding is assigned and with an official nod from senior management. This is the coherent, reasoned, rational process represented in advertisements for project management books and certifications.

Or, again, you could get thrown into the deep end of the pool.

Regardless of which of these scenarios is experienced, acknowledging the importance of a project manager's beginning actions is important.

The phenomenon observed with beginnings is the exponential impact misaligned beginnings have on project success. It's important to initially align on what everyone involved is truly expecting. Just because everyone accepts the project charter or gets an email string does not mean everyone has the same understanding.

How does that work? They are all speaking the same language and the project requirements have been written down and everyone agrees. Where is the ambiguity?

These are people. They all have different experiences and educational backgrounds. Many may speak English as a second language or are at different stages of their careers. Consider the interpretation and emphasis behind the words.

This activity benefits from excellent communication skills and the ability to *Speak the language* of those involved.

Now for a story. As an application engineer I worked with specification data sheets for electrical components. Characteristics were listed with corresponding values. "Accuracy: 1%" as an example.

This is a straightforward representation of how something would appear in a project. Everyone reading this understands the goal is 1% accuracy.

Now the questions begin. Is that a six-sigma or three-sigma number? Over what range of measurement? Is that a percentage of full scale or of reading? Is that number made up of gain, offset, and linearity influences? How were those tested? This is all the information making up that 1% number that not everyone may agree on.

When a project begins, key details—even those agreed upon—must be inspected for their potential impact on the project. Look beyond the words for intent: where did they come from, what is the practical outcome expected?

Ask questions. Think the project through. Meet with the stakeholders and listen carefully. The goal is to confirm alignment. If everyone involved is not speaking to the project in the same way, the beginning is the time to figure that out. Document and store that information in a place you will remember. Be thorough.

The beginning is also the time to define what the project is and to land these concepts with all involved parties to confirm consensus. Not six months into development.

OCD as a superpower

To be honest, my personality includes a little OCD. It is a useful affliction at times. My desk is organized. My work is documented and tracked in a notebook. Files on my computer are in order and updated. It drives me to organize and execute. Truly the superpower of project management.

A project is an organized effort to accomplish a task, and even those with OCD need to discipline their talent to be successful. Organization does not just happen. It is a skill to be developed. Observe and learn from others. Emulate what works.

The point here is that being organized is a continuous improvement opportunity. Invest the effort to develop the skills and you will never stop finding better ways to structure your tasking activities. And then you can enjoy the efficiency that will positively impact your project management efforts.

It's magic!

A fundamental concept of project management is the critical path. Determining the optimum path to completion is both a goal and a skill.

The concept of the critical path as a constant is a fallacy. The path to completion changes as the project executes. With experience, you develop insight facilitating dynamic reorganization of project activities to deliver a shortened critical path.

As the onion representing the project is peeled, so to speak, new options are revealed. Being mindful of these ever-changing opportunities opens up the possibility to delivering early, delivering under-budget, or to compensate for lost time and prevent being late.

This positive phenomenon comes from experience. It's a reward earned after years of project management efforts.

It is important for the project manager delivering *It's magic!* to know that others may not understand what you are doing. This is an opportunity for change management and managing of expectations. *Management cannot value something they do not understand* applies here.

Organize people

Communication skills are critical when organizing people. Getting contributors on board with the project will be an early project communications opportunity. There is also a constellation of management, interested parties, and gatekeepers, all with whom you must be to communicate.

Your ability to organize people will determine if you are able to successfully execute a project. Success hinges directly on your individual communication skills.

Organize information

Projects generate flows of information. Emails, conversations, meeting minutes. There are the official presentations and formal written updates. Information in a project is a lot like the classes taken in college. Most of it you will never use again.

A subset of all that information will be useful. And you will need it readily available sometime in the future. When the need arises, some people become experts in sifting through emails looking for what is needed or at scouring whatever storage medium holds the thing they are looking for.

An overlooked project skill is organizing the small bits of information shared on a regular basis. These are the technical expert insights shared in a meeting. A sentence in an email. Brief parts of the greater puzzle. Learn to recognize them when presented and have a method for saving them. One approach is an FAQ or Readme doc with each piece of the puzzle dropped into it. It keeps all the answers in one spot. It takes just moments to save these each time, but it delivers big when needed.

The avalanche of project information requires a written record. A memory backup of the project in process. Records of thoughts, spoken details, short term tasks to be executed. These should be written down and reviewed/updated regularly. Some prefer typing this into a document on a computer. Others write in a physical notebook. Preferences vary.

My understanding: Manually writing something reinforces memory. Typing, less so. This indicates that the optimal approach is to use a pen and notebook. The written record is the backup, and the act of writing reinforces retention. Over time, it is likely you will develop your own shorthand for your notes. The amount of writing done demands quality instruments: Notebooks sized to your handwriting. Fountain pens to reduce writing effort.

The goal is not to vacuum up everything in your notes. Use good judgment. Put some effort into creating a filter to determine what makes it into your notes. Don't forget the shorthand suggestion. My favorite is "FU" for "follow up." Depending on what is to be followed up on, the double meaning can add some humor to the exercise.

Organize information is a support function to *Close the loop.* Depending on the individual, executing the complexities of project management from memory is problematic. People *think* they will remember everything. In practical application, few possess the eidetic memory for such superhuman recollection. Hence, the invention of pen and paper.

Improved information organization can only improve your project execution.

Targets of opportunity

Put everything in priority order.

Establish project priorities early, because knowing their relationship to the critical path puts you in a position to take advantage of targets of opportunity.

Prioritization of tasks is important when there is more work than can possibly be done. Are you working on the right thing? Should a request be ignored due to insufficient bandwidth? Here is where those developed question-asking skills will deliver. Get the information needed to make decisions and define the path forward.

There are times when the planets align and people, equipment, time, money, etc., become unexpectedly available. Do not miss these rare opportunities. Keep the project organized, with a defined scope and requirements, and a demonstrable path forward. Then, when serendipity strikes and resources are unexpectedly made available, you can execute. The possibility then exists to deliver something in a short time frame normally impossible otherwise (*It's magic!*).

Another target of opportunity is the completion of short time-duration project tasks. Delivering a win like this provides a sensation of forward motion to contributors and management. Contributor morale is boosted because things are getting done. The leadership sees progress, which is always great. Multiple actions are closed out early, decreasing project complexity. You as the project manager now have a better feel for the project and increased confidence. If these project opportunities present themselves, take advantage. Everyone benefits.

All aspects of the project will not likely advance simultaneously. There may be parts of the project that are independent. This independence is a potential opportunity. You now have something that can be executed with minimal complexity. This is good for morale and the overall appearance of the project. Close out those short, easy-to-deliver opportunities early.

Watch for *Targets of opportunity* and be ready to take advantage of them.

Torpedoes in the water

There is a project management tactic that can help reduce the number of tasks requiring immediate attention. Many tasks require effort on the part of the project manager, but then there is a hand off to another contributor who must execute before the project manager must touch that aspect of the project again.

Sometimes this is called "the ball is in someone else's court," or less positively, "tossing it over the wall."

A variation on this is what I call "torpedoes in the water." By perceiving the time span others are actualizing part of the project as a feature, not a bug. Set up a project effort, remove obstacles, complete your input, and then schedule the next efforts. Hand off the task to the contributor. There will be a relatively predictable amount of time before you as project manager will need to re-engage with that particular responsibility.

The goal is a well-executed hand-off. Not the tossing of a "hand grenade" to next person.

The title for this approach comes from those movies where a torpedo is launched from a plane or submarine. Once launched, it just zooms through the water. The time between launch and the torpedo reaching its destination requires no additional effort.

While the "torpedo" tasks are running through other contributors, it frees up your time and mental energy to focus on other tasks. Now the project effort can run autonomously for some time. This is a great way to set up the progression of multiple tasks that are relatively short in duration (weeks, maybe a month) while freeing up your time for the more complex tasks.

There are specific differences between "toss it over the wall," "the ball is in someone else's court, and "torpedoes in the water."

"Toss it over the wall" is final. You are done, the work is all on others, and no feedback or further communications are expected.

"The ball is in someone else's court" indicates a lack of control. Decisions may be made by others and the tasks may or may not come back to you.

"Torpedoes in the water" has a defined beginning and destination understood by the project manager. Even though you have no direct input to the work in progress, you're aware of the next milestone and re-engagement is expected.

Getting things done

This chapter is a nod to what is found in "Check List" style project management books. Some organizational insights around project execution tangential to the people part of the project management equation.

Each is self-explanatory. Consideration may clarify aspects of project execution. Incremental improvements achieved though better organization of people and information.

CHAPTER 9

Get on It. Stay on It.

If you don't drive your business, you will be driven out of business.
– B. C. Forbes

Successful project management is not a passive activity. As a project manager, you must be engaged if you are playing to win.

A project management class was offered as an elective in my MBA program. Perhaps halfway through, the class discussion shifted to how to keep a project moving forward. Various software tools and documentation ideas were shared. The discussion was decidedly process-focused: Make sure the contributor team is properly structured, check. Analyze the project for the critical path forward, check ... blah, blah, blah. The concepts and approaches shared were passive without any engagement or passion. Tools are important, however, in the end, *people* get projects done. **Project execution requires human will driving skills applied to achieve goals.**

Project management is a leadership role. Leaders must initiate activity. Without this trigger, projects execute inefficiently and/or slow to a crawl. Sometimes they are even completely forgotten. Projects need a driver. And that driver is a human delivering project completion with an aggressive pursuit of the final goal.

Before we go any further, let's define "aggressive" as it relates to project management and completion. Aggressive is not bullying, violent, or rude behavior. Aggressive is the proactive application of energy to motivate people and drive the project forward. Everything will remain polite and professional.

Successful project management is an aggressive act.

Someone has to take ownership. Someone has to care. Passively filling in spreadsheets, sending emails, and holding progress meetings will not efficiently drive a project.

As in all things, moderation and awareness of what the human contributors find acceptable is required. Different organizations will support different levels of engagement and aggression. In some cases, those involved derive comfort from "ramrod"-level leadership, knowing someone is firmly in charge and driving the project to completion. The opposite is when only passive-level engagement is accepted. There is a whole spectrum of project-execution energy between these two points.

Passive-level project management engagement is the slowest and least productive. Unfortunately, this is the turn-the-crank style of project management popular today. A passionless process eventually delivering results with a quality reflecting the minimal human intellect and will engaged in the process.

The takeaway here is that engaging and investing in project execution as a discipline and the project itself delivers superior results.

Passion for the process and discipline

Project management needs determination and focus. It needs the will to see the project through to completion. It needs passion for delivering a complete project and meeting the objectives.

Engaging on this level can be challenging if the subject of the project, what is being delivered, holds no interest to you.

The solution here is to focus on your passion for the process, not necessarily the subject of each project. The process involves structuring the project. Efficiently executing through the steps. Anticipating what can go wrong and making contingency plans. Creating innovative solutions when the project starts to go off the rails. Successfully engaging contributors and ensuring a final, elegant delivery.

Burning out on projects: Projects come and go. One after another. Being passionate about every project has the real possibility of leading to burnout. Avoid this by maintaining passion for project management as a process. The discipline of the processes and watching your skills develop. Stay engaged on the project management as a discipline level.

Constructive persistence

Persistence: Firm or obstinate continuance in a course of action in spite of difficulty or opposition.

Once upon a time I was a calibration technician at a contract electronics manufacturer. One of the customers my employer manufactured for had transferred all their test equipment as part of the sub-contracting. One particular ancient, dilapidated in-circuit tester required attention from one of the customer's engineers on a regular basis.

The tester went down at an inconvenient time, as usual. That engineer worked all day trying to get it restarted. And then the next day. Three full workdays were spent troubleshooting. He worked through and eliminated each possible failure point, calmly executing his plan to root-cause the problem. This encounter inspires me to this day. It was professional persistence personified.

Persistence is repeated efforts over time in pursuit of a goal, and persistence is necessary to accomplish challenging tasks. Constructive persistence is an evolved, skilled approach required for successful project management efforts.

The observed phenomenon with persistence is the lack of understanding regarding the constructive part. Without a plan for the constructive component, interactions of an iterative nature become a source of frustration manifesting unconstructive behavior such as bullying and manipulations.

One of the joyless tasks required of a project manager is repeatedly following up on project details. Contributor communications not received when expected will need to be solicited so you can close the loop on project tasks. To track down these details, a project manager needs persistence tempered with a polite and professional approach. Just hammering away for an update will likely not generate the desired short-term results nor support a constructive long-term relationship with the target of this approach.

When you must repeatedly approach someone to get a response, it helps to vary the method of the ask. Email one time, voice the next. Try to weave the ask into other interactions. Change the structure and language of the ask. Use a positive tone. No one responds well to a monotone, semi-confrontational request.

These methods have planted whatever the ask was in their mind. Wait perhaps two or more weeks and reapproach. "Remember that thing we talked about a few weeks ago? I went back and looked at it again and the value is still there. We can still move forward. What do you think?" Since you gave the time to let their subconscious work through it, it may bring them to see the opportunity, I am not sure how or why, but this works more often than not.

An aspect of this phenomenon is people have a reset time after declining something. If you come at them too soon after the most recent ask, the outcome will be unchanged AND the undesirable response you received previously will now be reinforced. The duration of this delay time is unique to the individual and the complexity of the request.

And remember, persistence and antagonism are not the same thing. Don't be antagonistic. Make notes of all the little details that need to be followed up on. If a response is taking too long, make that call (*In person for maximum effect*). Remain polite and professional. Be a coach and advocate (*Be positive*). Provide guidance and offer support, but keep pushing for results.

When asked, sometimes a potential project contributor says no. Sometimes they say hell no. Sometimes they tell you to go to hell. It can get rough. Stay calm and professional. Do not burn bridges. This is just round one.

After the initial refusal, give the contributor time and space while you work on your plan B. Then go back for round two. Review your message and approach. Look for details that will resonate better with whom you are trying to influence. Enlist allies. Ask for insight from mentors. Stay calm and professional. Sometimes round two fails.

Start planning round three. This is an endurance and communications game. Never give up, but give the person you're trying to persuade space and time. This is very important. Do not wear out your welcome. The rookie mistake is to keep pounding away. That is counterproductive. The goal is to let your proposal percolate in their subconscious.

A consistent, professionally and politely delivered constructively persistent approach establishes project execution ground rules. Contributors will have awareness of expectations and engage accordingly.

A varied and skilled, people-centric approach to persistence delivers results.

Respect the people

Contributors are people, not resources or work-delivery robots. Be polite and professional. Say hello. *Say thank you.* Try to demonstrate having a personality. Make working with you interesting. Don't be a jerk. Stay positive.

If the roles were reversed, would you want to work with you?
Contributors understand when you check up on your project efforts. What they will not appreciate is, "Are you done yet, are you done yet, are you done yet?" No one likes that. Tailoring your update requests to what the recipient perceives as reasonable is important.

Different people have different update-request tolerances. Some should be checked in on every week. Others require a longer time frame to get some work done before you check in. Each person is different and figuring the time between checkups is a skill developed over time (*Constructive persistence*).

Being genuinely respectful is a skill. It is about acknowledging others' value as people.

What does respect look like? Don't interrupt people when they are talking. Listen to what they are saying (*Run silent, run deep*). Remember what was said. Respond in a timely manner (*Close the loop*). When scheduling a meeting, try to take into account your colleagues' needs.

Being respectful lowers stress and builds credibility. We could all use more of both.

The final piece of this puzzle is recognition. When someone makes a contribution to the project demonstrating dedication, extraordinary talent, or they just did a good job, you must recognize them. Bring it up in a meeting in front of leadership. If your organization has a formal recognition process, learn how it works and use it.

Genuine positive engagement will deliver short-term value to the efforts in progress. Long term, contributors will readily engage in future efforts with a project manager who respects them and they in turn respect

Bounded speculative paranoia

Only the paranoid survive.
– Andy Grove, Chairman of the Board, Intel

Why bounded? Without limits, paranoia, which is speculative by nature, is a mental illness.

A colleague once commented he thought I was more paranoid in my approach than anyone he had ever worked with. Not mental-illness level, but notable regardless.

That paranoia is the product of many, many experiences with projects falling completely apart. There are movie scenes where a train is crossing a bridge over a canyon and the bridge explodes. The train slow-motion falls. The locomotive plummets from a great height to a fiery end. I have had projects emulate that epic scene. These soul-shredding, grey hair–creating nightmares were also excellent, high-acceleration learning opportunities. A paranoid sixth sense is gifted from such experiences.

If you work on complex projects long enough, you will find yourself analyzing the project and the people involved, looking for where it can all go wrong and preparing contingencies accordingly.

Project management is an endeavor that rewards those who plan ahead. The opportunities for strategic thinking and reasonable contingency planning delivering value are practically infinite.

Bounded speculative paranoia will drive looking for the potential weak links in the critical path. Where can things go wrong? What actions can I take ahead of time to reduce the risk of that happening? Do I need a backup plan ready to go? This is a probability game of how likely it is that bad things will happen and what contingencies need to be in place to compensate. It's risk management that takes into account factors learned from experience and critical thinking focused on the reasonably possible.

Aspects of the project demonstrating *The free-association apocalypse* or *Unnatural conversation* characteristics benefit from *Bounded speculative paranoia*.

Speculative paranoia is an expert-level project management skill. It helps address several phenomena and is an important tool in the toolbox. Developing this skill takes time and self-review. Input from others on your approach is required to keep the efforts within rational bounds. Afterall, it is not called paranoia for nothing.

Balls in a tube

During a meeting where tasks are assigned, a contributor accepts working on a part of the project. The project manager is happy; this is an important task and the contributor agreeing to work on it is an ideal outcome. The conclusion is it will take perhaps two weeks to complete.

Four weeks later, with no contact or update from the contributor, the project manager follows up. Turns out another task was brought to the contributor. This task was perceived as having higher priority or was seen as more interesting. Maybe the task was prioritized because it was the latest request. Whatever the reason, the project manager has nothing to show for the passing of four weeks.

Someone more engaged got their work done instead.

The project manager assumed, since they had agreed on execution, the contributor was working on the task. This assumption is a common rookie mistake. The world does not work this way.

Everyone who is reading this recognizes this phenomenon instantly. We have all experienced this particular disappointment.

The explanation I suggest is the idea of *Balls in a tube*.

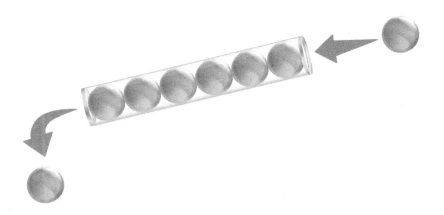

Visualize a tube or pipe capable of holding twelve golf balls. The balls represent work or actions assigned to a project contributor. Based on the N-1/matrix concept shared later in this book, each contributor's tube is already full of balls. There is no room for your project's work.

What to do?

Look for a hook. Anything that would motivate the contributor to work with you. For instance, is your project more interesting? Can you present the work as a quick and easy win? Can you show your project has a higher visibility in the organization?

One possible approach is that not all work assignments are created equal. If the discussion is just a brief "Can you work on this?" the contributor's quick reply will be "There is no room in the schedule." But remember, this is a matrix environment (see the chapter on N-1 and the matrix) and contributors have flexibility in the prioritization of the work. They may have opportunities present themselves from others after engaging in discussion and discovery (*In person for maximum effect, Credibility, Constructive persistence*).

When you are successful and the project ball is pushed into the tube, another ball falls out the other end.

This is where everything can go horribly wrong. Some contributors will agree, sometimes very quickly, to pop your project in. They do this because then you go away. After you leave, they pop it back out and get on with their life. Please remember, avoid insinuation when addressing these situations. Even if you are 100% positive this happened, you just smile and nod when you find out.

We arrive now at a secrets-of-the-universe moment in project management: Check up on your balls regularly. Keep your finger on the ball in the tube. No one should be able to take it out without you knowing. Most project managers move on when they get the ball in place. Lots to do and all that.

Be a do bee, not a don't bee.
– *Romper Room* television series

Stay engaged. Follow up. Check back, and progress will be delivered because the ball stays in the tube.

This also demonstrates to contributors you are paying attention. This is a useful reputation to have when engaging other contributors on other projects. You want to condition the team to expect regular follow-up. Be polite and professional but as constant as the north star. Over time, this consistent approach reduces friction in project management efforts.

Too simple? Yes, it is that simple. Monitor your critical project components regularly.

The immovable object versus the irresistible force

There are points in a project's development where specific aspects must be frozen in place until they have been completed. No last-minute updates or scope changes. Stick to the original plan and execute.

This is often related to a window of opportunity, defined delivery date, or resource availability. The milestone must be achieved without changes. There are always project-scope pressures. Small or large changes being injected for various reasons. Be mindful of the impact these will have on the big-picture delivery or critical-resource deployment. If there is a conflict threatening carefully laid plans, the immovable-object approach can be deployed.

Engage your supervisor constructively so they are aware of the critical situation and why making changes will impact the big picture. With that foundation in place, figuratively plant your feet and refuse to make changes. Be polite and professional. Fully disclosure and transparently explain the situation to all stakeholders.

Be prepared to deliver this explanation over and over again. There will be those who wish to influence scope in an unconstructive way. They will be persistent, coming back several times, perhaps with allies in tow. They will present varied arguments for why the project should be modified.

You must stand fast. Be the immovable object.

When deploying this strategy, it is important to have thought through the "why" in detail beforehand. Is this really the right thing to do? If you truly believe the project scope cannot be changed at this time for very good reasons, then stand your ground.

The irresistible force is the diametric opposite to the immovable object. This is a tactic applied when a straightforward ask is not enough. In many ways, the irresistible-force approach is a form of change management. A contributor is resistant or unable to collaborate. Resources are not available, etc.

The goal is to get a yes without strong-arming someone or pestering them to the point they no longer wish to work with you (*Constructive persistence*). Simultaneously, the goal is to portray the ask as imperative in order to get buy-in. The irresistible force is typically deployed over several engagements. Each engagement will require a different approach. New reasons, different allies. This is persistence writ large.

There is a spectrum of engagement from persistent to irresistible force. Beyond this, you have gone too far. Over-the-top persistence is going *Full kamikaze*, detailed below.

Deploy these strategies with care. Consider them expert-level approaches. But if you can master these, achieving the almost impossible becomes possible.

Full kamikaze

There is a point when persistence transitions from constructive to bullying. As a project manager, this will happen to you. Example: An aspect of the project is now frozen. A colleague wants to make a change. Even after a detailed explanation does not resolve the discussion, they continue pushing. It becomes obvious they plan on coming at you over and over until they get their way.

They are going *Full kamikaze*. They are taking persistence to a level that is no longer professional. It is transitioning to bullying. Where is this line crossed? My interpretation is between attempts three and four. Someone wanting change gets three tries.

Getting three attempts has some sort of special meaning to humans. If people are given the opportunity to attempt something three times, they are generally satisfied that everything that can be done, has been.

With the fourth attempt, there is a problem. Time is now being wasted. Three times declined should be the professional limit. Unless management is now weighing in, the discussion is over. The time for explanations is over. Tell them the decision has been made. Hang up on them if you have to, because they apparently cannot get the hint.

Or send them a copy of this book with this section highlighted. Why do people go *Full kamikaze*? Because it works. This form of bullying is quite successful. Just hammer the source until they give you what you want so you go away. Just as in the derogatory saying "Those who cannot do, teach. Those who cannot teach, administrate." Those who cannot develop effective communication skills, credibility, or leadership can always bully.

For many, *Full kamikaze* is sourced in frustration and trying to find a way to achieve forward motion. They finally arrive at a state of mind where they just hammer at the thing they want to move.

Conductors rule the world

Projects will be made up of many balls in many tubes. Orchestrating the forward movement of all of them I liken to the efforts of an orchestra conductor. The conductor stands in front of the musicians and waves a stick around. That waving of the stick provides cues for the musicians to follow. The conductor is not doing the actual work of the orchestra, making music, but if they do not do wave the stick around, the results are substandard. This is a people thing and just how things work.

A project manager has an element of conductor in how they guide the collective efforts forward. The critical path is delivered in a certain order and cadence. Communication is used instead of the conductor's wand. There are meetings, messages, and emails confirming balls in tubes are progressing in proper order.

This is an opportunity to develop your project manager prowess and grow from a rookie to a maestro.

Relentless, but in a nice way

This chapter was all about driving and maintaining project execution. The phenomena shared addressed aspects of the human equation in project management. The need for engagement and the constructive application of will and development of a proactive approach to keeping a project moving forward.

CHAPTER 10

The Fun Versus the Unfun and the Event Horizon

A contributor has been enthusiastically working on their part of a larger project. With every update meeting, progress is being demonstrated. The work is exciting and engaging. Then, not more than a few weeks before project completion, the progress reports change dramatically, no longer showing much in the way of progress.

The project manager asks questions and makes inquiries through their network (*Balls in a tube*). What has changed? Why has progress slowed to a crawl just as the project nears completion? What is learned is frustrating. The contributor's focus shifted to another project.

A direct conversation reveals the ugly truth. Attention shifted based on interest in the task. The less-interesting task was traded for the new and shiny one.

Everyone wants to work on fun and interesting things at work. There are always tasks more palatable than others.

This can help drive better contributor performance if the project is the shiny new awesomeness everyone wants to work on. People find time to work on the fun. Productivity soars.

Unfortunately, what is left behind is the almost finished and nearly complete. It's a phenomenon observed over and over.

This is the dark side to combining a matrix organization with an uninteresting or undesirable project. Once the fun has been squeezed from the opportunity, a matrix contributor has the flexibility to push the ball out of the tube and focus elsewhere. It's like when you replace chewing gum that has lost its flavor with a fresh piece.

Acknowledgement of this phenomenon provides the opportunity to strategize for this particularly challenging situation. When an opportunity to work on something sexier than the current effort presents itself, what comes next is understood.

The following are observed phenomena and ideas for addressing them, many of which manifest in subtle and remarkably irritating ways. **These are some of the more expensive phenomena from an organizational standpoint.** They prevent project completion just as an almost complete investment is about to be delivered.

How fun and unfun impact project delivery

Different aspects of the work experience have varied levels of appeal to different people. Certain tasks and engagements are desirable to contributors with an affinity for that specific work. Awareness of a contributor's interests is a skill worth developing. This will help identify parts of a project that may require increased attention from the project manager in order to prevent slowing of forward progress.

An important communication skill is presenting tasks in a way that avoids negative framing. The goal here is not to be Machiavellian and manipulative. You're looking to give a professional presentation of the work while excluding unconstructive and negative language (*Words matter*).

For many contributors, something new and short in duration is a welcome distraction. If communicated properly, small asks can be delivered almost effortlessly. The important thing here is presenting a clean, concise ask (*Now can you explain it?...*). Expecting a successful outcome from a poorly structured, vague, incomplete request is unreasonable. Several skills come into play here (*In person for maximum effect, Credibility, Perform due diligence*).

Most tasks within a project involve actual work. These activities are not terribly stimulating, but they make up much of the employment experience. As adults, we execute tasks of this nature regularly without a second thought.

Then there are those unstimulating tasks, onerous and undesirable, whose only reward for completion is that they reached their end. These are projects so ugly, so brutal and demanding, it is unlikely anyone wants to get involved. It might even be illegal to require participation.

One observed phenomenon is when a project manager is completely honest and transparent while communicating onerous tasks, and contributors buy in. Acknowledging the magnitude of the ask builds credibility. It also emphasizes the importance of the contributor as the only person who can make the difficult possible.

A story of an awful project: There was an opportunity to improve a piece of industrial equipment in a facility that thermally processed metals. The equipment being updated was critical to plant operation and could only be shut down for twenty-four hours maximum.

The available workforce was able to do the work, but it was estimated the time to completion could be twenty hours.

The team was gathered together and the ask was presented. It was emphasized that due to the long duration, participation was not a requirement. The reality of the situation was shared up-front. The work will be physically demanding, dirty, and just unpleasant. This frank sharing of the situation depressurized the team's anxiety. Everyone knew what a monster of an undertaking was ahead of us. The unspoken concerns had been spoken and confronted as a team. Twenty-two hours later, we finished. It was an accomplishment the team was proud of. A collective challenge overcome together.

A similar story, perhaps more an urban legend, is when Sir Ernest Shackleton advertised in the *London Times* for men to join his next Antarctic expedition. "Men Wanted: For hazardous journey, small wages, bitter cold, long months of complete darkness, constant danger, safe return doubtful. Honor and recognition in case of success." According to Shackleton, the response was of such magnitude it was as if the whole of London wished to join.

These two examples show an approach to characterizing less-desirable activities as unique challenges. It would be wise to sparingly draw from this well. Otherwise, you risk team burnout.

Regardless, when the truly awful injects itself, there is a potential path forward.

Being conscious of what contributors perceive as fun versus unfun is important. Structure your communications and follow up (*Constructive persistence, Balls in a tube*) accordingly. Developing expertise in this space can only improve your project management performance.

The 98% problem/Finish what you start

Hey! I'm no one's messenger boy, all right? I'm a delivery boy.
– Shrek

Project completion is the goal. On the first day of college, you receive the list of classes you must complete in order to graduate. Four years and thousands of hours later, if you are one class short, you will not graduate.

Projects are much like this. The delivered value from achieving 98% completion is likely not much different than 0% completion. Delivering 100% is what is needed. That minimum viable project must be delivered and that is likely 100%. A car without tires is 98% complete but until the tires are installed that car is not going anywhere.

The phenomenon observed: It is apparently human nature to be distracted or slack off just before crossing the finish line. Project after project, employer after employer, it is like clockwork. As the project nears the finish line, keeping contributors on target becomes increasingly difficult. The type of project, business, and education level of those involved change this experience not one bit. This phenomenon is as inevitable as death and taxes.

When a project nears completion, there will be a collective shift of focus. Everyone involved will begin looking to their next activity. This will result in a dramatic decrease in the project's forward momentum. Without foresight and discipline, that last 2% of the project will take as long to close out as the first 98%.

What to do? Watch for the change and be ready to mitigate.

Drive projects to a complete delivery. The project manager does not have the privilege of shifting focus as the collective effort concludes. Stay focused as the project nears completion (*Get on it. Stay on it*).

Have good visibility to whatever makes up that last 2%. Clearly define these final responsibilities and deliverables. Increase the tempo of updates. The project manager's engagement ramping up at the end of a project will help keep the greater team engaged.

Unrealized assets

An unfinished project is an unrealized asset. Investing time and resources in chartering a project, executing on a project, and then not delivering is dereliction on the part of the project manager, representing real failure.

The unrealized asset is not just the hard assets purchased for a project and left incomplete. Nor is it the cost of the project contributor's efforts that never come to fruition. The real loss is in the opportunity cost.

What was the expected value from delivering a complete project? Or from another project if the resources had been applied to completion?

No one puts money into opportunities to then receive no return on investment AND have their originally invested money forgotten. This is what happens when projects are not completed.

There is a psychological impact as well. Contributors derive satisfaction and professional development from completing tasks contributing to project success. Projects that never deliver deny them this experience. This will negatively impact future efforts.

Project managers are not just responsible for project execution. They are responsible for the money spent, contributor cost spent, opportunity cost of the money spent and contributor time, AND the ROI the project is to deliver.

Project management is that important.

The event horizon

People can only comprehend or consider a limited amount of time looking forward. I have taken to calling this *The event horizon*. Everyone's individual forward looking time threshold is different. Success in project management will require understanding your personal capability as well as those you work with.

An experience to share: A new project is kicking off, with work happening at the customer site. On day one, a colleague and I arrived to inspect where we would be working. Seven pallets stacked with components were waiting for us to install. The project was scoped with two weeks to completion. My co-worker was new, and the amount of work expected for just the two of us to deliver, in only two weeks, was causing him anxiety. He shared his concerns with me. I had not considered on-time completion a potential challenge. From my viewpoint, the project size and duration was reasonable. This is an example of two people confronted with the exact same project situation yet having two very different reactions.

This concept of an event horizon is important to project management. Human beings have limits when it comes to future planning. The observation shared here is that an individual's event horizon in planning over time is based on individual characteristics, experience, and personality. Experience and the use of project-tracking tools can improve on the individual's inherent talent.

A project manager must be able to comprehend the time frame of project execution. If a project is being managed by someone whose personal time horizon is shorter than the project/task they are managing, their stewardship of the project will be less than optimal. The inability to comprehend project execution over time increases project friction.

Similarly, when the number of projects exceeds a person's ability to track them all. Project deliverables cannot be optimized or even may be missed if they are not properly tracked. People can physically feel when this situation occurs as anxiety and stress arise within the project.

The event horizon concept applies to contributors as well. Task execution over time distances beyond an individual's event horizon ability will inject friction into project execution. If a contributor is the sole source of needed skills but the time frame is causing problems, try breaking up the project into pieces. These shorter-duration tasks can then be linked at a later date.

Requiring an individual to operate significantly outside their event horizon sets them up for failure. Trying to force a fit with a contributor with regards to the event horizon will not be constructive. The project will not benefit. Your relationship with a colleague will suffer. Worst-case scenario: The contributor gets broken by an ask far outside their ability.

Differences in how the time-frame aspect of the project effort is viewed can result in hearing the easiest word to say in the English language: No. Sharing a future state that requires a longer time horizon than the individual you are making the request from is capable of, they will not understand your request. And "no" will be the answer.

An observed sub-phenomenon of the event horizon phenomenon is how workload impacts the event horizon. Increasing levels of tasking will eventually reach a tipping point. Above that threshold, adding to the workload will begin decreasing an individual's event horizon. This can have unintended consequences. Previously scoped work will be more difficult to manage. The perceived competence of the project manager may be negatively impacted. Project execution may be less skillful than typically enjoyed by the greater organization. This is related to the *Problem with mountains* phenomenon discussed later in this book.

The event horizon concept applies to both the project manager and contributors. Awareness is the first step in developing the skills addressing this phenomenon's impact on project success.

Taking into account individual time-frame capabilities will improve project performance.

Out of phase

Misunderstandings come up within a project if aspects of said project are being discussed by two people who are approaching the situation from different places within the project.

As a writer, I have a wholistic view of creating a book, which has stages of activity. The rough draft comes before beta review and multiple polishing reads. Then the professional edit is followed by the final review. If I share the rough draft with someone for a critical review, as the writer, I am looking for commentary on characters, story, and flow. What I may get back is a critique of grammar, sentence structure, and punctuation. What I needed and what was received are not in the same phase of the project. We did not communicate properly, so we focused on different stages of the effort and, as a result, time has been wasted, with no useful work delivered.

If the project manager is asking questions and performing due diligence to prepare for an effort others assume is already complete, all kinds of misunderstandings occur.

Perhaps a good analogy is a long email string. If you are looking at email number four and replying while the person(s) receiving your response are already on email number eight, it is likely the communication will be challenged.

Similar to making sure you are *Speaking the language*, it's important to be aware of where others are in the project process and to keep ongoing activities aligned.

Personality

INTJ Death Glare
– Characteristic INTJ facial expression

For years, colleague's, friends, and family would ask, "Are you angry?" My reply, "I am not." Apparently unwilling to let it go they would restate, "You look angry." To which I would again reply, "I am not." They would persist, "Are you sure? Because you really do look angry?" My reply, "I was not angry but I am getting there now."

This exchange happened over and over again. Then one day I was looking up information on INTJ's as that is my location on the MBTI. Someone commented about the INTJ Death Glare. So I did an online search. What people have been asking me about for years is common to all INTJ's.

Fun fact: Every children's cartoon villain is based on the INTJ personality type. Children are taught to hate and fear INTJ's from day one.

If you are interested in the Myers-Briggs Type Indicator (MBTI), it can also help with guidance on the time-scope visibilities based on personality.

There are those whose event horizon and capacity for strategy is excellent (INTJ). Others are a natural for people to look to for leadership (ENTJ). There are personalities that are born cheerleaders (not INTJs). Some have a predilection for communicating and connecting with others (extroverts). Potential leaders who can read people (ENTP).

As a project manager, awareness of the strengths and opportunities for improvement derived from personality are worth exploring. The goal here is not a Machiavellian power trip. Consideration of colleagues' common humanity contributes to a positive work experience. It also delivers opportunities for synergies and the corresponding productivity improvements. A true win-win for everyone.

Learning about personality and developing the skill to evaluate those you engage with every day can only bring you success.

This is not my first rodeo

As projects increase in size, complexity, duration, and technical requirement, so does the need for increasingly skilled and talented project management become evident.

In addition to skills, experience brings understanding of how projects execute. A seasoned veteran will remain unflappable when the project inferno rages and the collective effort is threatened. They already have a plan.

A project manager's experience delivers a singular characteristic to the effort: calmness. Project execution, deadlines, and challenges will generate anxiety and other unconstructive emotions in participants. Undamped, they can begin to resonate and affect performance. A calm hand on the wheel really helps in these situations.

Since everyone has to start somewhere and the needed experience comes from, well, experience, consider adding a little stoicism to your project management demeanor. Be (or fake being) a calm, even-tempered persona providing the rock that others need during the never-ending challenges of project execution.

This phenomenon of experience is both obvious and misunderstood. The idea that experience delivers value is obvious. *How* it delivers that value is often not obvious. And the need for even-tempered project management is worth exploring.

The things you know you know

There are things you know you know. Budget, available contributors, project charter ... these are all straightforward. You know the foundation for project structure. From this, you can evaluate the more difficult aspects of the project.

Defining and considering the aspects you know give the project structure and points of reference (*Asking good questions, Perform due diligence*). It will also reveal aspects of the projects requiring further definition.

What you know gives confidence and the path forward.

Once this concept is acknowledged, experience will lead to an epiphany: realizing there are things you know you don't know ...

The things you know you don't know

There are things you know you don't know. For example: a vendor's real delivery date. You have the expected date of delivery on the quote, but when it actually will arrive is unknown.

Then there are time estimates versus what the final outcome will be. And estimated cost versus final cost. Categorizing these undefined loose ends is a sort of risk analysis. In most cases, awareness is what is needed so you can react if the unknowns go out of tolerance. Define limits with an associated probability.

Often, a source of misunderstanding can be identified at the beginning of a project. Start by asking questions probing for the clues. The questions have their roots in experience and are targeted at aspects of the project demonstrating an inordinate complexity or vagueness. This type of inspection will reveal project details not likely to support success.

Example:

Step 1: Deliver the proposal.

Step 2: Organize the team.

Step 3: Something magical happens here.

Word to the wise: That step 3 warrants further investigation. *Bounded speculative paranoia* delivers value in this space. This is a gap in turn-the-crank style project management.

Determining what you know you don't know is the foundation for risk analysis. That risk analysis leads to contingency development and improved confidence. These are all things a project manager must be proficient in to facilitate successful project delivery.

The things you don't know you don't know

Anything that can go wrong, will.
And at the worst possible moment.
– Murphy's Law

Engineering minus sales equals scrap
– Anon

No book on project management is complete without Murphy's Law. It's as immutable and constant as gravity and the speed of light. It is twelve words representing the purest truth.

Now for a story about the things you don't know you don't know.

A long time ago, in a land far, far away, there were two warring kings. With the kings evenly matched, their war was without end. Both sides could bring the same number of archers and knights to the field. Neither's swords and arrows could break the stalemate.

One day, a salesman came to the gate seeking audience with one king. He was ushered into the throne room to make his pitch.

Before the salesman could speak, the king bellowed, "I hate salespeople, and I am far too busy for this. Begone!"

The salesman graciously bowed and left.

He then traveled to the other king.

This king glared and said, "I hate salespeople, and I am very busy. You have five minutes."

The salesman bowed and then began his presentation. "Thank you for your time, Your Majesty. My presentation will be short. The opportunity I bring to you today is a new invention ... the machine gun."

This is an excellent example of a disruptive technology being introduced.

Spending a few minutes to think about and inspect those things you don't know you don't know can positively impact your project. With enough project management experience, this concept will be felt at the core of your being. This is all the stuff that comes out of nowhere and derails even the best-laid plans.

We should separate acts of God from this discussion. If force majeure is involved, it is likely that no amount of speculation would have helped. Barring asteroids destroying civilization, there are a host of project requirements that will not be visible at the beginning of a project.

Is a critical piece of test equipment due for calibration right when testing is planned? Is a key subject-matter expert retiring in the middle of the project timeline? It is likely no one has considered this or would think to volunteer this information.

There will be things negatively impacting project execution that cannot be planned for. However, with experience (and a little *Bounded speculative paranoia*), risk mitigation in this area is possible.

That is what has been going on?

This chapter shared the phenomena around how people's likes, their personality, experience, what is known and unknown and when are important considerations in project management.

A project manager's and contributor's forward looking time abilities will be important to project success.

Managing interest levels in different parts of the project will play a role in successful project execution.

The inevitable shift in focus just before the project reaches its conclusion should be anticipated.

Investing thought during the project's genesis in managing knowns and unknowns has its benefits.

Each of these is a big concept. Proficiency here will make an equally big improvement in your project execution.

CHAPTER 11

The Process Apocalypse (Frankenstein Processes)

Any man can endure adversity. If you wish to truly test a man's character, give them power.
– Abraham Lincoln

Life is tough, but it's tougher if you're stupid.
– John Wayne

The road to hell is paved with good intentions.
– Proverb

The government should pay people to dig holes in the ground and then fill them up.
– John Maynard Keynes

Why look for conspiracy when stupidity can explain so much.
– Johann Wolfgang von Goethe

This chapter title is accurately descriptive, if somewhat inflammatory. Here, you'll learn about processes gone wrong and the human phenomena driving these opportunities for improvement.

The coming example first needs some background.

Spreadsheets are synonymous with processes. This is why they were created—as a paragon of process efficiency and productivity. Even the most basic use of spreadsheets delivers benefits appreciated by all.

Unfortunately, there is also a dark side to spreadsheet processes when they transform from valued productivity tools into time-sucking vortexes of soul-destroying frustration.

Projects all make sense in the beginning. Starting out with good intentions: a well-thought-out effort addressing a compelling need.

Then it all goes horribly wrong.

This is where the story begins: I start a new job that includes pricing custom or semicustom systems made up of complex subsystems and components. All the work is done in spreadsheets, and the process is fairly straightforward: Put quantities in certain cells and the spreadsheet math does the work. The final sales price is the output.

There was a small selection of "standard" offerings. All other systems were à la carte with many, many options. In the à la carte tool, it is possible to select everything making up a "standard" system.

The idea behind the standard system was for it to be a lower cost option versus à la carte. These being the most popular selling product, standard was an established system. It was advertised as shorter delivery, less upfront engineering. A quick and easy choice.

While reviewing the spreadsheet's outputs, I began comparing the standard offerings to the à la carte and found à la carte was much less expensive. With the customer tendency toward getting a "standard" quote AND an à la carte quote, the optics on the approximately 25% standard product premium were not constructive.

My first thought: What a brilliant sales strategy to increase profits! We're steering customers to the standard offering through the implication it is the easier, faster, regularly manufactured version (implying lower risk).

Perhaps it would have been a brilliant strategy if it were true.

Upon further inspection, what I found instead was a spreadsheet passed from person to person, and each new owner had made changes to the formulas involving pricing. For the most part, these were added, undocumented, multipliers. The result was an impenetrable morass of interlocking, irrational math formulas arriving at a price structure neither rational nor possible to explain.

This is how Frankenstein processes are created.

This dysfunctional outcome was not arrived at by design. There was no malicious intent. Regardless, a point was eventually reached where the process failed. Or at the very least, uncertainty and inefficiency were added to the point that they virtually killed the activity they were supposed to govern.

Phenomena around process can be the most difficult to identify AND the most difficult to change. The goal of this chapter is to break these phenomena up into more comprehensible pieces. Then build out the details in a manageable way.

Managing process phenomena is a heavy lift for a project manager. Developing expertise in this space will deliver reduced project friction.

The Frankenstein dysfunction in real-time

A project manager will not be able to see a bad process until after the project is executing.

Real-time identification of dysfunctional processes is critical. Otherwise, frustration at the inability to achieve goals will begin to impact project cohesion. No one wants to work on a death march of a project where you are fighting process instead of doing actual work.

Be ready for *The process apocalypse* phenomenon, and have the tools ready to prevent the situation from speed-bumping the project. This is not about *if* it will happen. This is about *when*. Knowing this will happen—and that it is not unique to your personal experience—reduces the stress and anxiety when it does. Your success lies in developing the tools to engage and resolve the challenge.

The visibility that project management gives to all aspects of the project is not a shared experience with the other contributors. As project manager, it is possible you will be the only person to identify the process as the problem. Most project participants are doing work, not determining whether what is being done is a good idea.

Sensitivity to the differences between a higher-than-expected workload versus a poorly structured process is key. Adding people can address both gaps. But only one of them delivers added value.

Inefficient processes are legion

Created long ago, their origins shrouded in the mists of time, most processes governing corporate activity are legacy creations. The phenomenon experienced over and over is that although everyone executes through processes, no one, and I mean no one, is reviewing, updating, or innovating processes.

Processes are often built from older processes, with no critical review performed on their arcane machinations, ever. Working these ancient, poorly documented, and equally poorly understood work streams is the ongoing nemesis of project management.

Why do these inefficient, energy-sucking fossils still govern so much in the corporate world?

Because changing them is both difficult and very unsexy. Fundamentally unfun, high risk, and high effort are involved. The only reward: a thankless change-management effort of monumental proportions.

No manager ever maxed his bonus cleaning the stall that is legacy processes.

If you are working through a byzantine, life-sucking process and wondering why?

Now you know.

There's gold in them thar hills

This is a continuous improvement opportunity separate from the projects you are working on. For those with masochistic tendencies and iron will, legacy processes offer an opportunity of truly magnificent proportions to satisfy your continuous-improvement itch.

Shining a light into the dark corner of legacy processes is oddly not intuitive. This is not something people gravitate toward. Review the legacy processes your projects are executing through.

Finding these nuggets of pure gold in process improvement will not be difficult. Regardless, once the "gold" is discovered, the magnitude of the dollars returned to the company's bottom line will be impressive.

Reduce complexity, eliminate unnecessary activities, document, and clarify. Expertise in this rarified space will deliver value. With experience, higher-value improvements will become apparent.

I would like to make a short statement here for clarification. Looking for bad processes is something people do not intuitively gravitate towards. However, once the idea to look for bad processes' manifests, the actual work of inspecting and finding is easy. Bad processes are everywhere. The challenging part is the actual work of updating and fixing bad processes.

Management cannot value something they do not understand applies when updating processes. Strategies and skills for change management and managing expectations, plus everything in chapters 1-4, are required.

Finding the opportunities for improvement will be easy. Executing the improvements requires real skills. And nobody likes change.

You have been warned.

The project production possibilities curve

Just like the production possibilities curve taught in every economics education opportunity, there is a project production possibilities curve. This is the theoretical maximum rate of project delivery if optimal alignment and efficiencies actualize as planned.

Then there is reality. Project management executes through processes. Processes are often less than optimal. The greater the process challenge, the less optimal the delivery.

Processes are subject to external influences. Say a critical component holding up the project arrives early and the project gets an unexpected leap forward. Or a completion date is discovered to be inaccurate. This give and take during project execution dynamically moves the delivery relative to the project production possibilities curve.

Project management experience and skill development improve delivery relative to the project production possibilities curve. So stay engaged. Accept the things you cannot change, but be vigilant for those serendipitous opportunities to jump ahead *(Targets of opportunity)*.

Everything presented in this book is an opportunity to shift ever closer to realizing an optimal project production possibilities curve.

Who thought this was a good idea?

I sense a disturbance in the Force.
– Star Wars paraphrase

How to identify processes gone wrong?

If the thought, "Who thought this was a good idea?" keeps popping up, that is likely a sign.

Here are some other signs: Forward motion unexpectedly slows. Completion milestones need pushing out. A little voice in your head whispers something is wrong.

Acknowledgement of this phenomenon and experience develop awareness. Exposure to bad process eventually elicits an almost Pavlovian response.

And then they tried to fix it . . .

Do not attempt to include bad processes fixes as part of the project they are impacting.

A bizarre form of *Hooking on* is the attempt to leverage ongoing project execution to update a process. It's when a process problem becomes visible and the idea to "update" the process is brought to the project participants attention.

This distraction of "fixing" the process becomes the focus instead of bridging process issues to keep the project moving. Be on guard for this. This can be doubly troublesome when complexity-focused people start winding up an IQ test style, complicated upgrade to the process (next chapter: *Smart people think complicated is fun*).

Fixing a process is a project in itself. Do not subject your project to the scope creep that process updates become.

Make it fit?

Perhaps poorly defined and poorly understood processes are best approached as opportunities? Use the lack of process definition as a way to minimize complexity and accelerate the project? Figure out the minimum requirement to honor the process and execute?

This approach is not about cheating or a lack of integrity. This is about rationally dealing with the process's poor fit, lack of rigor, obsolescent aspects, and/or right-sizing the process effort to the task at hand.

What is really needed? It is important to meet the minimum process requirements in a way that can be explained. This will protect your credibility.

Then eliminate the nonsensical and time-wasting make-more-work steps that add no value.

My go-to approach? Identify the situation and master the game. Aggressively hunt down the tricks and traps early and work through them. Be transparent (*Management loves surprises!*). Document and communicate what is being done. Taking *Liability, the project killer* into account is important to keep contributors from overreacting to changes. Taking everyone to an uncomfortable place in process execution should be avoided.

Unrealized potential as far as the eye can see

Be prepared to identify process apocalypse scenarios as they occur. A real-time strategy to communicate and provide guidance to the team will be needed. The goal here is to acknowledge the phenomena and guide the project through the process obstacles with minimum losses.

CHAPTER 12

Project Execution: An Exercise in Masochism?

Here be dragons.
– Common medieval-era map notation

Some project-execution phenomena are injected into projects by people who don't know they are doing them. This adds increased complexity, decreased efficiency, and stress for everyone.

These phenomena are not obvious nor intuitive. Explaining them to colleagues or management is not a straightforward activity. Many are accepted common practices, and pointing out their problems is not a path to endearing yourself to others.

Pointing out to a colleague that they practice one of the phenomena presented in this chapter may not have a positive outcome.

Attenuating the influence of these phenomena is worth it. Do not expect it to be easy, though.

Tread lightly.

Distraction elimination

The story:

A plant engineer had multiple projects in motion and six direct reports to execute them.

An executive manager was fixated on old, unused equipment. He believed that money could be saved by pulling spare parts from the junkyard. The plant engineer knew it was all valueless garbage. Unfortunately, this was not a constructive message to share with an executive.

The junkyard of long-dead machinery proved itself a distraction over and over again.

The executive would grab one of the direct reports and reassign them to trying to resurrect some piece of junk. That direct report would then not complete tasks previously assigned. There was no constructive way to deflect the executive's attention.

That left what is perhaps a passive-aggressive solution: Eliminate the distraction.

Every day for the better part of two or three months, the plant engineer's day started out with a cutting torch and a fork truck, spending a few hours filling dumpsters with scrap steel.

With the junkyard gone, the executive stopped re-tasking people.

Distraction eliminated.

Distractions abound in the workplace, and people do enjoy a good distraction on occasion. This is doubly so in the self-deterministic world of the matrix organization. Telling someone to not do something is never a winning solution.

One possible solution is removing the distraction. Once it's out of reach, the focus, perhaps with some encouragement, will fall back to where the project needs it.

The likelihood of a distraction causing a problem within your project depends on the individuals involved. Some people lose focus easily. Others are sensitive to certain distractions. Once you acknowledge the phenomenon in general, the skill to see when it is happening will manifest naturally.

Angels on a pinhead

A mathematician asked the question "How many angels will fit on the head of a pin if the first angel is half the size of the head of the pin and each subsequently added angel is one-half as big as the previous?" The answer: an infinite amount. This also represents the time it takes to accomplish anything when this approach manifests in project management.

If there ever was a reason to bring back good old-fashioned flogging or the pillory, it would be this method of task management. Opinions may vary, but this is where I land on the subject.

This popular approach to managing workload is a monumental waste of time. When I first encountered it, my reaction was, "Who thought this was a good idea?" That was soon followed by, "We must stop doing that."

The story: Management meetings were held one Saturday morning each month. This gave the team an opportunity to meet without participants being pulled away by day-to-day events in the factory. The team met in a conference room, and at one end of the room was a whiteboard. This whiteboard had a list of perhaps twenty in-progress projects around the facility. Each project had progress notes and an expected completion date.

Each month the project list was reviewed and efforts were shared.

This exercise in re-prioritization made no sense to me. Company resources (money, time, and people available) only supported working on perhaps three of these projects at any one time. Yet, in these meetings, prioritization of all twenty was reviewed and changes were made (*The ABCDE incidence*). Incomplete projects just short of completion would often be reduced in priority (*The 98% problem*), the efforts and expense expended since the last meeting reduced to a loss if the project never got prioritized again. Prioritization often changed based on the need to advance projects that did not demonstrate progress since the last meeting.

Let me say that again: Prioritization increased based solely on the fact that the project did not progress in the last month. It was a decision not connected to any business reason (*Show me the money!*).

Instead of delivering any one complete project, incremental progress was spread across the entire list. Result: a year going by with nothing completed.

This was my first glimpse into the nightmare that is the *Angels on a pinhead* approach to project management. Most humans cannot process more than a few goals at any one time. This limit also applies to teams working together.

If the to-do list is too big, contributor and management attention shifts over time. The likelihood of shifting decreases with experience. Writing down a list of twenty or more possibilities confuses people and impairs their decision-making.

Using *Angels on a pinhead* with a matrix organization creates a time-wasting engine delivering inefficiency on an epic scale.

It cannot be emphasized strongly enough that *angels on a pinhead* is a terrible approach. It is demoralizing for human beings to work like this. Nobody completes a task without switching back and forth, over and over.

The only benefit to this approach is the project manager can always say "it is being worked on" while being able to demonstrate some incremental progress. Nothing is ever in the backlog. There may be progress to report at every project update, and no one ever has to deliver the message that no progress is being made on any task. This approach dispenses with efficiency, responsiveness, and productivity for political expediency.

A factor that amplifies the inefficiencies of *Angels on a pinhead* is that the longer a project is executing, the more likely a meeting will be called and the scope and/or priority tinkered with (*Manager's prerogative, The ABCDE incidence*). This possibility increases the risk of delays or outright non-completion.

Doing everything at once is the best way to achieve the least progress. If the goal is maximum inefficiency, *Angels on a pinhead* delivers.

So how does the *Angels on a pinhead* phenomenon manifest? In any of several ways. There are project managers who are tasked with more and more projects. Instead of focusing on the key efforts that are reasonably deliverable, an attempt is made to show continuous progress on all projects.

These project managers forget that resources are finite, perhaps limited to ten working contributors, for example. If the project list contains more than ten opportunities to execute, how do you divide up the team's efforts?

Perhaps prioritize and execute one contributor for each of the top ten projects. Maybe double up contributors on certain larger or higher-priority deliverables.

Or you can begin assigning fractions of contributors' time. They can work 30% of their time on one project and 70% of their time on another. As additions are made to the project list, the number of fractions increases in number while the effort available to each task shrinks.

Now, how can you keep the awful phenomenon from occurring in the first place?

Discipline. You must apply old-fashioned gratification-delaying discipline. Do not be distracted by the new shiny thing. Have that serious discussion about what is possible and not possible. The ability to stay the course is the skill needed (*Immovable object*). Prioritize two to five goals and park the rest.

Project delivery will accelerate due to the dramatic increase in efficiency. The bad news is, at some point, management may question why you have unilaterally changed the "doing everything all the same time" approach to a tight focus on a limited number of projects (*Management cannot value something they do not understand*). Prepare for this change-management opportunity. It may be useful to share this book with them.

The rookie mistake here is to go straight to management and bluntly tell them they need to limit the number of asks they present to the organization. This is not a constructive approach.

Management will be more receptive if you demonstrate improved efficiency, lower costs, etc. (*Be positive, Show me the money!*). Communication skills will be key to your success.

Addressing *Angels on a pinhead* is a change-management exercise. There is no silver bullet presented here, but even small incremental improvements will deliver results that can be surprisingly dramatic.

Multitasking can cause brain cancer

The phenomenon of multitasking is at the root of the inefficiencies demonstrated in *Angels on a pinhead*. Multitasking increases project-execution times dramatically.

Getting things done requires focus. Alternatively, there is an energy and focus tax on switching tasks. If you want to finish that slide presentation in the least amount of time, you must stay focused, without interruption.

Emails and instant messaging are the worst productivity-tax enablers. Switching focus from a task to an email and back decreases productivity. It is likely not possible to avoid these situations, because most people reading this book perform literally hundreds of different tasks in a day. Like the other project-management phenomena shared, the goal here is awareness.

Awareness of the cost of task switching will help you identify the problem and keep the multitasking under control.

Some tasks require exceptional focus, time, and imagination to complete. Learn to identify and plan for these, because to achieve a high-quality delivery, these high-talent-input tasks should be scheduled so that they are not interrupted.

Start a task, finish a task. This is the most efficient way to execute tasks within a project. Often this is not possible, but acknowledge the challenge and leverage this understanding to improve project success.

Smart people think complicated is fun

> *A problem cannot be solved at the same level of*
> *intelligence at which it was created.*
> – Albert Einstein

Amen, brother.

Complicated approaches are easy for bright, talented people. Stand on your left foot, say supercalifragilisticexpialidocious while patting the top of your head with your right hand ... no problem. IT is the poster child for this phenomenon. Impossible-to-find controls. Non-standard language. Gaps in explanations where it is assumed the listener knows the "simple" stuff.

The smart people are not being malicious. For them, this really is easy. And maybe even a little fun. They enjoy working through all the obscure and inconveniently located steps in a process. Afterall, what is the point of having smarts if you don't explore their limits? Or if you don't share your intelligence with others?

For those who are not "in the know," these interactions are frustrating. The smart people are not trying to make things difficult. Honestly, they are just doing things the best way they know how and having a good time doing it. They genuinely do not understand the complexity is not well received by others.

This phenomenon takes patience (*Constructive persistence*) and a lot of *Speak the language* to get through. When these smart people share information, write things down, because what is being shared will likely follow no rational pattern. Keep them talking. Listen carefully. In conversation, smart people will say valuable things. Smart people associate "important" differently. Their assignment of value to information will likely be different from yours or others. This makes it difficult to just ask for that important stuff (*Asking good questions*).

After acknowledging this phenomenon, it will be obvious when it happens.

Jiggling the handle

Jiggling the handle is a variation on the *Smart people think complicated is fun* phenomenon. This phenomena manifests in both products and processes. They are often created as an artifact of *The 98% problem*. They actualize as irritating and obscure interactive features. If there is any level of complexity involved, expect *Jiggling the handle* to manifest.

A customer is using a product. Its performance is not as advertised. They contact the manufacturer. The solution is an undocumented setting impossible to find without the subject-matter expert explaining. This is called the "jiggle the handle" fix. People "in the know" just make the change. Flip a hidden switch. Slap the side of the machine. Cycle power. Sacrifice a chicken. Whatever. Anyone else watching the undocumented, non-intuitive effort required is disturbed by it and shakes their head. *Who thought this was a good idea?*

Processes can have similar struggles, where some aspect is poorly documented and not user-friendly. Everything works as intended, then at some point there is an operation required that is neither intuitive nor even possibly rational. Something was left unfinished or the customer experience was not a factor in the development process. Please keep in mind that the smart people who created this situation do not see complexity the same way. Nor do they assign importance the same way. This is a communications and guidance opportunity.

Jiggling the handle configurations can snowball as technical debt builds up until almost no one can figure it out. These cascaded, overlapping, multiple interactions are best avoided. Remove "jiggle the handle" characteristics from your projects as quickly as possible.

Once you are aware this phenomenon is common, you too will see it all the time.

It's too big

How does one eat an elephant? One bite at a time.
– Hindu saying

That which does not kill us makes us stronger.
– Friedrich Nietzche

When it comes to exceptionally large, long, and/or complex projects, these two quotes capture some of the philosophy in dealing with them.

Sometimes it is overwhelming. Too many parts in motion. Too many undefined aspects of the project. Too many information requests unanswered. It can get to be a bit much.

You are not alone. Every project manager at some point is handed something that looks so big, complicated, and undefined that it unnerves them.

Have patience. Get some quiet time. Write things down. Organize things. Address one aspect of the project at a time. Other times, walk away for an hour, do something else. And then come back and re-engage. After some mental inspection, the shape of the project will emerge and the path forward will become visible.

Stay patient; don't give up. You are not the first person to find yourself in the headlights of an oncoming project. Keep working on managing these situations skill. You will get better at it after being run over a few times.

Problem with mountains

Completing something is an important part of contributing to a project.

This phenomenon is about the perception of the work assigned as endless and unstimulating (*Fun versus unfun*).

Dumping endless, never-to-be-completed work on a single individual is unconstructive. The party line: This maximizes output because there is no possibility of anyone running out of work. Butts in seats looking busy and all that.

Shoving endless work at people is not an optimal approach. Human beings need to finish what they are working on. We get that shot of endorphins when delivering completion. Be aware of this, and structure the work so they can see the light at the end of the tunnel. Productivity and engagement soars when completing things is part of their work experience.

Break up the work, switch in different tasks, personally help out. These are approaches that can help execute a particularly unsatisfying part of a project. Make sure no one contributor is getting all the least inspiring work. When possible, mitigate those unfun challenges.

More work than ever can be done

This is about the project manager's work prioritization of the never-ending avalanche of things vying for your attention and not to be confused with *It's too big* or *Problem with mountains*.

Likely, if you are reading this and engaged in project management, there is literally more work in your task list than you can ever be expected to complete. This result comes from a combination of *Manager's prerogative* and N-1 implementation.

The military uses work overload in officer training. Officer candidates will be assigned a long list of tasks and requirements to achieve during their training. They receive demerits for each incomplete or improperly completed task. Enough demerits and you wash out of officer-candidate school. There are literally more things to do than you could accomplish if you gave up sleep and did nothing but work twenty-fours hours a day, seven days a week.

How do they pass and graduate? By making choices between what can be ignored and what must happen.

Project management can require some of the same calculus. What is really needed?

Making those prioritization choices is a skill that improves with practice.

That is not right

This chapter presented phenomena commonly practiced. They are even often accepted. Complexity and inefficiency introduced as a feature, not a bug.

Political considerations manifesting phenomena impacting project management. Unimaginative assignment of tasking. Smart people being smart people.

Even small efforts to address this chapter's phenomena will deliver tangible, high-value outcomes.

CHAPTER 13

Welcome to Thunderdome

This chapter is about change management and continuous improvement.

Why do people do what they do? Why do they do anything at all? How do you convince someone to do something? What if they do not want to do something? And why is "no" everyone's go-to word?

"No" is the easiest word to say. It delivers a high return in avoidance with virtually zero effort invested.

"No" is the most difficult word to overcome. Once a person says no, the effort to change that response to a yes is several orders of magnitude greater than was expended in saying no.

Getting past no is better achieved with a plan. An observed phenomenon about no: Some people think they can walk up to someone and just keep talking until they get a yes. Barking at people is not a skilled approach; it is coercion and bullying.

Constructively engaging no and positively achieving a mutually agreed upon yes require skill.

Why skill? Because risk aversion, the word no, and people's inherent resistance to change are complex challenges.

Change management

A story about why people do what they do: A young technician is disagreeing with a senior manager. Like with many young and left-brain-focused people, the communication is less than constructive. They are disagreeing on a change required by the manager. The technician says, "You are making me do this." The manager shakes her head, saying, "I cannot make you do anything. The only actions I can take is to sign your paycheck and call the sheriff to have you removed from the building. Everything you do here is voluntary on your part."

The point of the story is that in the workplace, nobody "makes" anybody do anything. There are levels of coercion possible through disciplinary action and threatened termination. These are explicit when HR is involved and implicit when a more-senior person directs an action. This is how hierarchy works. None of those approaches are an option for most project managers.

That leaves us mere mortal project managers with influence and change management. How do we convince others to accept change? Or even better, support it?

This is where those developed communication skills are going to pay off.

Relying exclusively on the merits of your proposed change opportunity may be successful with more-engaged project contributors (those who see the value in spite of your clumsy communication attempts). Unfortunately, hoping a good idea shines through a poor execution of communication is not a reliable strategy.

The path: Acknowledge you cannot make people do things. Understand you have limited authority to push change. Forego bullying as an option. Stop hoping the good idea is sufficient motivation on its own. Look to communication skill development and strategize your change efforts.

All this change-management communication takes time. What if there is no time to work through the change-management process? Perhaps there is an immediate need and the contributor must act now. If time is of the essence, authority is needed to prompt immediate action.

Understanding the need for a skilled approach, combined with visibility of almost every phenomenon shared in this book, is a start. Now, go develop your change=management expertise and reap the rewards.

The easy button

For an approach that increases success, deliver the easy button. Make working with you, and on projects you manage, as friction-free as possible.

There are two potential sides to the easy button. Organizational and rational.

The organizational easy button is delivered without unnecessary complexity. Plan out frustrating delays and misunderstandings. Organize project information, ask questions and get answers, process details addressed ahead of time (*Now can you explain it*). Get approvals ahead of time, remove obstacles. High speed, low drag.

The rational easy button is about reducing injected stress. Address contributors' *Liability, the project killer* up front. Run interference on political aspects. The value of what is included in the rational easy button changes from person to person. A custom-tailored approach addressing individual needs can be advantageous here.

Any effort rationalizing project execution is generally welcomed. Building the easy button is a demonstration of competence, and project participants appreciate this (*Credibility*).

A popular response to a well-delivered easy button: "That is all you need?" Contributors are often genuinely surprised when they encounter this approach. A straightforward ask that allows them to efficiently accomplish something while demonstrating their competency? With a clear path to a shot of endorphins at project end? Sign me up.

Having project tasks prioritized and defined in advance is important. It's the proverbial easy button. Everyone wants to work with the easy button. Be the easy button.

Like a glass of cool water in a desert, the easy button is received especially well by those frustrated by politics and complexity (*N-1 and the stretch, matrix*).

How laziness can be useful

If you want an especially difficult project completed as quickly as possible, assign it to a lazy manager. They always find the shortest path to completion. – Bill Gates

The useful aspect of laziness is looking at a task and being willing to question "why." Why should we do this? Why this way? Is there a better way that takes up less of my time?

Lazy people question expending effort.

Having a limited few hard-working lazy people in the organization is a force multiplier.

Laziness is intolerance of inefficiency and solutions lacking elegance or insight. Lazy people are fundamentally skeptical.

But why is lazy that useful? Because lazy people are skeptical efficiency-seekers.

The corporate poster child for success is an extroverted, high-energy, constantly in motion go-getter, continuously taking action. They must be seen doing things at all times.

That kind of personality is not sensitive to opportunities to use less energy. They have a tendency toward working harder, not less. They overcome challenges by expending more energy.

In an environment populated with these energetic, hard-working, driven managers fearlessly engaging difficult challenges to prove their value, a lazy manager will find a target-rich environment of low-hanging, easily delivered value.

Not everything has to be that hard. Sometimes it is easy.

This phenomenon is shared as an insight. Something to think about.

The bigger hammer

Angels on a pinhead is a bigger hammer approach. Increasing workload while decreasing output. The solution most arrived at? More people are needed. Or people need to work longer hours.

If a little is good, a lot must be better. Working harder, not smarter.

There are elegant, efficient solutions. An enlightened, considered development of project objectives, contributors, and resources through the skilled application of experience and intellect. A path forward everyone involved will be proud to participate in.

Then there is *The bigger hammer*: too much work or too much overly complicated work for the desired outcome. A fundamental understanding of the task and its execution is missing. In some cases, it is a legacy artifact of *How we did it in the old days* (see below).

The bigger hammer is a common outcome of big picture solutions. Attempting to realize an epic vision without taking into account the details.

Regardless of the source, if the thought coming to mind is, "There must be a better way," then this may be an opportunity to add some innovation and intellect into process improvement. Apply some laziness and enjoy the increase in productivity.

The silver bullet improbability

Some who picked up this book had the thought to look for the secret to getting things done. To learn "If I just do this or say that," their projects will start executing flawlessly. Perhaps a checklist or the magic phrase "Open Sesame." My personal go-to comment: "Sprinkle some fairy dust on it," or "pull a rabbit out of my hat."

They want the silver bullet to making all their project efforts deliver on time and under budget.

That kind of silver-bullet thinking is an impediment to success in and of itself. Just as having a goal of the perfect delivery is not going to happen (*The crap/perfection juxtaposition*).

Silver bullet–seeking can be driven by too many *The bigger hammer* experiences, including frustration with tasks and project work requirements spiraling out of control. It's a reaction to symptoms driven by a lack of expertise in organization, communication, and subject matter.

Each phenomenon shared in this book is an opportunity for developing skills, shifting the probability for success just a little bit more in your favor. No one skill or strategy will deliver absolute success. There are no silver bullets here.

Stop looking for silver-bullet solutions and do the hard work of developing your portfolio of project management skills.

The long game

Sometimes polite and professional does not get it done. It happens often in a project that has a contributor who is not on board with the project. Sometimes this is a critical contributor. Regardless of making them aware of the project's charter and visibility, they have other priorities or are not inspired to participate (*Insufficient gravitas*). Or they may just not like you (*They are a peach; Prima donnas*).

This is a tough situation. The contributor is typically someone you do not have authority to compel. What you do have is a polite and professional request (*Constructive persistence*). If that does not work, you have a problem. Running to your supervisor or their supervisor will not play out well with your colleagues. Even if that person is then compelled to participate, there is a real possibility that passive-aggressive tactics will follow.

My humble advice: Stay calm and play *The long game* (*Run silent, run deep*; *Be positive*). Either this project is going to happen or it's not. If it is green lit by your superiors, regular progress reports are likely needed. Never call out the contributor who refuses to engage. Just share in the readout that certain actions are delayed due to conflicting priorities. Give the person who is not on board yet the opportunity to correct their lack of vision.

Keep the obstacle front and center but low key. Give them time to figure out the optics that their lack of engagement will bring up. Wait for your supervisor to ask, and then calmly—and in neutral language—explain the situation.

Eventually, their reluctance will become a bright neon sign, flashing, "I am not a team player."

The temptation to *Unleash the fury!* here will be almost overwhelming. Being forced to play *The long game* is the result of a contributor's unprofessional behavior. View these experiences as an opportunity—even a test—of your ability to professionally engage and drive success. Even when the inferno of frustration rages.

There are two goals to accomplish in these reluctant-contributor engagements. One is the execution of the current project. The other is to get your long-term relationship on track.

Despite the contributor's injection of unneeded extra drama, it is important to understand you will work together again in the future. This is why we play *The long game.*

Short-dog syndrome

My first experience with the short-dog syndrome phenomenon was in the military. Basically, people who are grouped together for tasks will keep their focus until close to the end of the task's time. It also comes up when people are retiring or have resigned but will still be around for the obligatory two weeks.

Perhaps this is the root cause of *The 98% problem.* Once the end of their association is close to ending (two weeks seems to be the most common time frame), social cohesion breaks down.

The closer the exit date becomes, the less focused people become. In addition to being less helpful or responsive, belligerence may rear its ugly head. There is a perceived opportunity to air past grievances without fear of repercussion. Most people are not aware they are exhibiting this behavior.

Knowing this phenomenon is going to happen takes most of the stress out. Get what you need before hitting those two weeks. Be ready for some unorthodox behavior. When you aren't surprised by it, this phenomenon is relatively manageable.

Losing that new car smell

When you are new to an organization, everyone wants to meet you. When engaging with colleagues on your first assignments, every request is supported and every question answered. Then, several months later, the responsiveness drops precipitously.

There is a honeymoon period where everyone supports the new person. The length of this time varies from organization to organization. Your professionalism and likeability will extend or shorten this time.

What to do about this phenomenon? Don't be a burden (*Asking good questions*). Be polite (*Say thank you*). Take advantage of the increased engagement to build bridges and meet people (*In person for maximum effect*). Learn as much as possible.

Awareness that the good times will soon come to an end helps. Plan for the transition. Leverage the temporary high-engagement opportunity for future success.

Next level insights

This chapter builds on previous ones. Phenomena already shared and the skills developed from those insights are needed to engage change-management opportunities.

Change management is pervasive to the project management experience. Skill development in this space is a life-long effort. Each marginal increase in ability will deliver success.

The Easy button is a concept where the project manager can pre-package the ask to optimize acceptance and speed of execution. This requires more effort up-front but increases contributor engagement and output.

Laziness is a misunderstood skill. In today's high-energy drive to success work environment being sensitive to, and critical of, energy expended delivers low-effort success. Specifically in the prevention of *The bigger hammer.*

The focus on silver-bullet minimum effort, perfect solutions is a delusion bordering on being a mental health issue. Silver bullets do not exist. Do the hard work of skill development.

There are people phenomena that cannot be resolved in a short time frame. With an eye to keeping a project on track and the need to preserve a path to maintaining long term relationships. *The long game* is a possible path forward addressing these challenges.

Short-dog syndrome and *Losing that new car smell* are both time phenomena. When someone is new and when individuals or groups are getting close to ending their time working together.

Take what was shared here and increase your project management capability.

CHAPTER 14

Thank God Someone Knows What They Are Doing

A man's gotta know his limitations.
– Dirty Harry

There is a story that is perhaps an urban myth. This was back in the 1970s. A company acquires a large mainframe computer—the kind so massive it takes up the space of a modern server room. This wonder of technology makes the company money. Real money. Executive level-visibility money.

One day, the computer stops working. Company technicians and engineers work for a week straight without success. An engineer from the mainframe manufacturer is brought in. By the end of the second week, things are getting tense. Management bonuses are in danger, and the CEO is now personally involved.

The manufacturer's engineer pulls aside one of the company engineers to share a possible path to resolution. There is this guy who just retired who is really good at fixing these things. He might be worth bringing in. This bit of information works its way up to the CEO. The nod to proceed is given.

The retired engineer agrees to consult and is flown in. Arriving on-site, he takes stock of the situation, asks some questions, and flips some switches. Then he starts opening up the panels containing the computer, its peripherals, and all the wiring. After looking around inside for a few minutes, he then asks for a screwdriver. Leaning back in, he tightens something. After closing up the panels and a short trip back to the main controls, he flips a switch.

The computer rumbles to life. Revenue can flow again. Consultant's total time on-site: forty-five minutes.

An elated CEO says to the consultant, "Submit your bill and it will be paid immediately."

A few days late, the bill arrives and is brought to the CEO for approval. It has a single line item: a charge for $1,000. This is a lot of money in the 1970s for less than an hour of work. Itemization of the bill is requested. The consultant re-submits the bill: "$1 for screwing lose screw, $999 for knowing which screw to screw."

The bill was then paid.

An important detail often left out of instruction in project management: expertise. Identifying the need for, and engagement of, subject-matter experts.

There are technical subjects and processes that present themselves when a project is being considered AND during project execution. They require specific expertise not in the project manager's skill set.

Engaging subject-matter experts as a project contributor or for ad-hoc input is a project management activity (*Asking good questions, Now can you explain it?, In person for maximum effect, Say thank you, Speak the language, Credibility, Allies, Be positive, Liability the project killer, Left brain versus right brain, Constructive persistence, Respect the people, Smart people think complicated is fun*).

Develop your subject-matter-expert engagement skills. Collaboration with experts is part of the project management experience. Awareness and polished communication skills are key to success in delivering success.

What are experts good for?

Subject-matter experts know things.

They can do things.

And they have done things in the past.

When a project's existing pool of talent is the gap preventing progress, resolution requires expert input. There is a need to include others as project contributors or to bring your questions to someone who has the needed expertise.

Subject-matter experts are experienced colleagues focused in a particular area. They represent a source of knowledge that project managers will be going back to over and over.

This may have to be done as the project is executing in order to prevent the gap from speed-bumping the project. *Asking good questions, In person for maximum effect,* and *Credibility* will play important roles here.

The communication challenges experienced in these engagements can be especially taxing (*Smart people think complicated is fun*). *Unnatural conversation* can rear its ugly head. Be ready to gently, with tact, guide the discussion back to the task at hand.

My experience: Subject-matter experts are typically enthusiastic about providing their unique support. There are exceptions, but people so far down the knowledge rabbit hole as to be considered Subject-matter experts are not threatened by sharing their knowledge. They are also very enthusiastic about the subject in which they are experts. That is why they put so much effort into becoming an expert. That enthusiasm drives them to want to share. That's a positive trait shrewd project managers leverage.

For many subject-matter experts, their contribution is a demonstration of skill and value to the organization. It is an affirmation of their usefulness. Being the only person who can make something happen is a nice ego boost.

Oddly enough, subject-matter experts rarely demonstrate the challenges associated with *Insufficient gravitas*. Apparently, when you have real talent, deep skill, and knowledge, concerns about associating with less-important people is not an issue.

Word to the wise: Experts are often senior members of the organization and well-connected (*Insinuation and gossip are verboten*). In addition to providing expertise, there is likely a fantastic networking opportunity to be had.

The people you are reaching out to are specialists, highly skilled and experienced. Polite and professional is important (*Say thank you*). Try to be interesting and make the interaction frictionless and maybe even fun. If possible, do not burden them with resolving menial or mundane details and chores (*The easy button*). When possible, present the challenge in a way that demonstrates mutual benefit. Take into account *Liability, the project killer* in these engagements.

Some rare subject-matter experts are not willing participants. Or the path to engaging them is not straightforward. People with the skills qualifying them as a subject-matter experts are in demand. Project managers may have to compete for a slice of the subject-matter expert's bandwidth. This is another of the hundred-plus situations when communication skills deliver success.

Word to the wise: There is value in letting subject-matter experts ramble (*Run silent, run deep*). They know more than they know they know. If you are listening carefully, important details will be inadvertently shared. At the right time, leveraging these bits of valuable information can deliver amazing things.

Constructive professional relationships with subject-matter experts are a necessity. Develop those subject-matter experts engagement skills.

How we did it in the good old days

The phenomenon here is when experienced contributors steer project goals based on past performance. Prevent nostalgia-driven project outcomes. Awareness to the potential for this happening and having a strategy to mitigate it is the message here.

Experienced colleagues sharing past outcomes is a good thing (*What are they good for?*). Institutional knowledge is valuable (*The things you know you know*). Use reminiscing about events and *Asking good questions* to build a more robust project. The current state has roots in the past state. A conversation in this space delivers value.

Do not let *How we did it in the old days* set the path forward. Experienced, long-standing employees are valued contributors. The goal is to leverage their skills and experience while maintaining a fresh perspective.

Identifying obsolete approaches that creep into a project due to contributor nostalgia and comfort level is a skill. Maneuvering these unconstructive influences back out of the project (*Immovable object, Change management*) is the needed complementary skill.

These are challenging engagements. The colleagues pushing nostalgia are often more experienced, have been with the company longer than the project manager, and in many cases are subject-matter experts on the topic.

It takes a sophisticated toolbox to manage these situations (*Asking good questions, Now can you explain it?, In person for maximum effect, Speak the language, Credibility, Perform due diligence, Allies, Be positive, Constructive persistence, Respect the people, Smart people think complicated is fun, Change management, Building bridges*).

Successfully preventing *How we did it in the old days* from infecting a project is an expert engagement. A project manager needs a robust portfolio of project management tools in their toolbox to be successful in this space.

That time I was the receptionist for a billion-dollar company

It can happen that *you* are the needed subject-matter expert. Or you're the person others network with to support their success.

As an application engineer, I worked for a company that supplied electronics for a large construction-equipment manufacturer whose annual sales were over $1 billion. Every three weeks I flew out to the customers and spent the week working on-site.

Different parts of the customer's organization did not communicate with other parts well. It was made up of quality, production, two different engineering groups, and the service group. The service group and engineering had a particularly high level of animosity between each other. The relationship was dysfunctional to the point that people were comfortable making it public that they refused to speak or work with each other.

Over several months I developed my role as go-between and resident expert for these different groups (*Building bridges*). Long-term challenges were solved. I dealt with serious quality and development issues. One after another.

The section title referring to my being the receptionist for a billion-dollar company? My presence and contribution with this customer was so universal and constant, I enjoyed unescorted access to the entire facility. It was like I was a senior manager with run of the place. The receptionist would hand me a badge and I was good for the rest of the week.

One day I walked into the main lobby and the receptionist and I exchanged pleasantries. She then asked me to stay for a few minutes while she ran an errand. I was to explain to anyone coming in that the receptionist would be back in a few minutes.

For five minutes, if you walked into that lobby, I was your greeter.

Your chocolate is in my peanut butter, my peanut butter is in your chocolate

Building on *That time I was the receptionist for a billion-dollar company*, the phenomenon shared here may be the basis for the consulting industry.

The story:

A customer's new product design was not performing to specification. Development was falling behind and visibility had been escalated. My employer was the supplier of a key component identified as the source of poor performance. The sales manager supporting this customer demanded engineering support to prevent the situation from turning into a debacle.

This prompted a customer visit from the sales manager and myself. Our arrival was greeted by THE subject managers in the design of the customer's product. Brilliant and representing decades of experience, the customer's engineering team was made up of global leaders in their field. They had thoroughly investigated and documented the problem and presented this information for review.

The shared documentation demonstrated that the problem was real. The customer's application was not performing properly.

It also quickly became evident that my employer's components' basic design and physics could not be the source of the problem. How was this conclusion reached? Because as the application engineer, I was the subject-matter expert for the component—so I knew what I was talking about. It also helped that U.S. Army radio-repair school developed me into a troubleshooting Godzilla.

For many, this would be the end of the engagement. Inform the customer it is not your problem and get an early lunch.

Rookie mistake.

Figuring out the problem does not originate with your employer's component is the low-engagement answer.

The opportunity here is to help figure out what is actually happening. After figuring out my employer was off the hook, I shared steps to take to isolate the issue. The observation shared: The performance issue is firmware, not hardware.

A week later, confirmation came that it had been a firmware math error.

The complete story that came out after the fact is that the customer had a hardware development team and a firmware development team. Both competent and capable. But when something did not function correctly, each team started blaming the other. Without a mechanism to break the deadlock, this could go on forever, one side claiming the other's chocolate is in their peanut butter. The other side saying no, your peanut butter is in our chocolate.

When these project management situations happen, paralyzing deadlock can be the result. How do you resolve this when teams point at each other as the source of the problem? And how do you do it quickly before damage to relationships occurs? Or even worse, management begins inserting themselves into the situation (*Let's figure this out before the adults get involved*).

The customer's solution was to bring in a competent third party (the supplier) and make it their problem. They act as a semi-neutral arbiter, providing suggestions to break the deadlock.

The observed phenomenon here is that project contributors who are peer-level may experience a deadlock situation. Resolution may require a third party. This could be an SME, the project manager, management, or, as in the example, an external resource.

Be prepared for the *Your chocolate is in my peanut butter, my peanut butter is in your chocolate* situations. A polished resolution delivery will minimize emotionalism. This is an opportunity to lead through the challenge.

Mission impossible

There are times when project managers cannot find a needed contributor or answer. Information sources available, reaching out to colleagues, even leadership, fail to deliver. The project manager's Venn diagram does not have a solution inside the circle. More is needed. Perhaps a *Then there are the things you know you don't know* situation.

It's nearly impossible to find a subject-matter expert for an answer without knowing upfront who to find. Situations like this are perhaps similar to sales cold-calling. Time to play the Mission *impossible* theme song and think outside the box.

Is there a need to bump into someone who might be able to point you in the right direction? Perhaps a meeting you must invite yourself to? You will likely be engaging a string of people you have never spoken to before. Each of those interactions must be positive while asking for information and encouraging the sharing of the next step in the search.

Perhaps you do not even have a single colleague to start with. Time to look through the company directory and reach out.

Yes, contact people you have never spoken to before.

This begs the question: **Have you ever thought about how others experience meeting you for the first time?**

This *Building bridges* opportunity will be an expert-level demonstration of communication skill.

You'll need smooth, positive communication skills combined with sensitivity to the situation and the need to not burden the person you are randomly reaching out to.

How can this possibly work? As long as you are polite, interesting, and do not wear out your welcome (*Forty-three seconds*), your unexpected reaching out breaks up the day for whoever you are speaking to. It can be fun for them if you do it right. They literally get to be the hero, providing that one thing no one else could.

Contacting people without introduction through others is not for the faint of heart. Work on this in small steps. Mentoring benefits this skill. Developing this solo might be a bit much.

Should you master this skill, your project management capabilities will have truly grown.

The light-bulb electrician

The problem is with the flux-capacitor. Perhaps the knuter valve is out of adjustment and your jiffler bearings need blinker fluid. Once those are resolved, there is still the problem with the Hemway. What the hell is a Hemway anyway? About five or six pounds.

The above non-sensical string of technical-sounding details, if spoken with confidence, will mislead those who are not experts in the subject. Just look up "retro-encabulator" on the internet.

On occasion, in your search for contributors with specialized skills, you will encounter self-proclaimed experts who are not really experts. These are the so-called light-bulb electricians because they only know how to change light bulbs. They survive by virtue of work history and providing their underwhelming expertise to people who do not know any better.

From a project management standpoint, this is a challenge. The low-capability subject-matter expert may be the only contributor for some aspect of the project. It is also likely you will have no authority to make a change. What to do? Minimize the impact of their incompetence on the project (*Perform due diligence, Allies*). Scrutinize their every input (*Ask good questions*).

Don't confront them on their incompetence. If they have survived this long, they likely have friends in high places—or their longevity gives them a credibility you likely do not have.

Be polite, be professional. Many of these people have egos starkly out of proportion to their level of talent. Recognizing the situation early on and planning the limits of their involvement will clarify the project's path; it will also minimize negative outcomes related to incompetence-inspired missteps by a mislabeled subject-matter expert (*The long game*).

I know a guy...

This chapter delivered insight into subject-matter-related phenomena. Where and when they are needed. The need for subject-matter expert relationship development. Some of the more extreme approaches needed at times finding a critical person to collaborate with.

The concept of leveraging subject-matter experts to break project deadlocks is detailed through several phenomena.

Subject-matter experts challenges to watch for around nostalgia injected into project efforts and so-called experts.

Sometimes what is needed to move the project forward is to know the right person.

CHAPTER 15

Secrets of the Universe Revealed: N-1, the Matrix, and Project Management

Having this chapter at the end was a tough decision. In the corporate environment, so much of the project management experience is tied into these two concepts. Both of these organizational approaches are presented in an MBA program, and my experience is that the practical impact this has on how things get done in the resulting environment is not represented anywhere. Everyone is left to "figure it out." Hence the Groundhog Day experience of project management phenomena.

Despite the matrix organization having been implemented decades ago, most people still operate in a hierarchical mindset. People tell people what to do. Like parents telling a child how to behave. A workplace hierarchy functions differently than a home hierarchy. Are there similarities? Yes. Enough for a young person entering the workforce to enjoy a fundamental understanding.

From that basic start, effective engagement in a professional hierarchy can develop.

Unfortunately, professional hierarchical proficiency does not prepare anyone for the N-1 and matrix experience. A structured hierarchical worldview is misleading to those who have not been clued in on what the matrix is and its practical implications. Much has to be unlearned before the complexity, flexibility, and demands of navigating the matrix can be understood.

Each phenomena presented previously, and the potential tools for those situations, stand on their own. But when combined and applied in the N-1 or matrix environment, additional opportunities become apparent. A portfolio of skills addressing project management phenomena realizes profound synergies in the N-1/matrix space.

Now for the finale.

N-1 and the stretch

If you take some business classes or go through an MBA program, at some point the concept of N-1 is introduced. This philosophy of labor management involves determining the number of people needed to perform work and providing one less than estimated. The theory being this will produce tension and stretch the people doing the work to achieve maximized productivity.

Corporations large and small universally implement N-1 in a variety of forms. It is unlikely that anyone reading this book is not at least to some degree operating under this philosophy.

The implementation of N-1 has practical real-world project management implications.

In N-1, all potential project contributors are fully loaded prior to project launch. There are no spare resources or people waiting for work to do. Not only do they have a full-time load, but there are additional stretch items stacked on top. This is the *Balls in a tube* phenomenon. There are a lot of balls laying around and no empty tubes for them to go into. Without acknowledgement of the N-1 environment and a plan for engaging it, the project management experience is problematic.

The observed phenomena affecting project management in the N-1 environment appear to be largely misunderstood. Awareness of the N-1 philosophy impact on initiating and managing execution of projects is critical.

Remember, there is more work than available people, equipment, and money. This is by design. It is a feature of N-1, not a bug. Management has structured it this way. Do not view this as an obstacle. And forget about complaining, N-1 is not going away. Time to drink the Kool-aid and get on board the N-1 train. Learn to embrace the suck.

Navigating N-1 will require excellent communication skills, professionalism, and a positive attitude. Everyone you interact with is very busy. They are not looking for problems or complications. It is important to understand the human part of the contributors you are seeking to engage.

The human factor is the in-between space. There are processes and project charters to the left of me, execution to my right, people in the middle. N-1 must be considered when strategizing your people approach. There is so much efficiency and synergy to be found in this human space. This is also where the N-1 effect can hopelessly derail your project if you are insufficiently sophisticated in your project management approach.

Acknowledgement of the N-1 phenomena, self-analysis, and skill development is the path forward.

The fully loaded N-1 condition interacts with another experience in the corporate workplace: the matrix organization.

What is this matrix everyone says we are in?

The matrix organization is the end result of hierarchical flattening, grouping of similar skill sets as shared resources, and the push for self-organizing teams.

This section presents the observed phenomena of the matrix and project management in the corporate environment. A detailed exploration of the matrix is not presented here. Others more knowledgeable than I have created myriad books, class, seminars, and many other resources to improve your knowledge of the official matrix-approach party line.

The flattening of many companies' hierarchies results in a "pool" of skilled workers who are expected to collaborate effectively without distinct leadership or lines of authority (*The self-organizing fallacy*).

Many modern skills can be efficiently shared across the organization. Perhaps a company does not see enough CAD work in individual departments to justify dedicated CAD people on a department-by-department level and instead implements a "CAD group" as a shared resource.

As in N-1, the human element is amplified in the matrix environment. The practical matrix dynamic is individual contributors with significant autonomy over which tasks they will address and in what order. Or even at all.

This autonomy has profound implications for project managers engaging contributors for a project. Take some time to really think about how this unintended matrix autonomy actualizes in the real world. There are different levels of individual discipline and interests. Personality conflicts. The time investment in one-on-one negotiation.

Here is where this gets interesting: As previously explained, with the universal implementation of N-1, everyone is fully loaded and then some with stretch goals. Now combine this with the autonomy of a matrix organization. People with more work than they can ever do AND they have influence, overtly and covertly, over what tasks they will perform. The introduction and execution of projects in such a contributor environment will not be a straightforward process.

Thus, when a new project is introduced, there are no resources available (*N-1 and the stretch*). And as you work through the process of negotiating one-on-one with each project contributor (*matrix*), the failure to close the deal with even a single participant will doom the project.

But wait, there's more …

Some contributors interact as if they are not in a matrix organization. Did their supervisor give them the signal to support this project or person? No? Then that contributor does not have time for you. This is not how a matrix organization works. That is how a hierarchical organization works.

This is where the line in the project management job description "Able to influence others and accomplish goals without legitimate authority." comes from. Successfully managing a project is not just a technical exercise in determining the critical path and executing. This brief line in the job description defines the people-skill requirement.

Realization that the N-1 and matrix phenomena impact project management was an epiphany in my own project management journey. With the N-1 phenomenon, awareness and guidance on how to engage this more complex environment is critical. Without it, project managers experience endless frustration.

An observation: N-1 and the matrix require project managers with above-average organizational ability and critical thinking skills. Negotiating the crush of N-1 and the matrix while simultaneously delivering real project work is not for beginners.

Some organizations develop robust project processes in an attempt to compensate for N-1/matrix challenges. These well-defined processes will benefit from understanding and acknowledging the people space. People are doing the work. And it is likely the people part was never taken into account in whatever software app, spreadsheet, or written project process that was implemented.

Contributors working in the N-1/matrix environment are not looking for another burden. Polite and professional is the rule. Stay positive. Everyone is working hard, and being negative or a jerk won't help. Don't insinuate or be passive aggressive. Project management is for adults.

Acknowledging the N-1/matrix phenomena and developing a sophisticated approach will improve your project management delivery.

The matrix strikes back (the international matrix)

Outsourcing is the most visible aspect of the international matrix. Grouping skill sets and activities enables moving the work where it is most financially advantageous.

The typical N-1 and matrix phenomena remain applicable in the international space. The respective tools implemented may require modification to successfully engage the international matrix.

Collaborating with international contributors is its own unique challenge (*International communications*). *In person for maximum effect* is not an option. English as a second language can be a real obstacle. *Liability the project killer* and *Angels on a pinhead* phenomena may be more prevalent.

The quid pro quo discombobulation may enter into the equation. You give me something, I do something for you. This is problematic in the matrix environment.

It can also be useful.

Facilitating an international colleague's communications and requests within your own region or facility becomes the currency to pay for what you need done.

A few exchanges like this can support *Building bridges,* and you can get past the zero-sum game.

The project management phenomena in the international setting are the same as phenomena everywhere else, though phenomenon emphasis and magnitude may change. Take the time to learn the differences and strategize future approaches accordingly.

The shiny-object distraction

Contributor autonomy in the matrix environment and N-1 work overload create susceptibility to distraction. The N-1 work overload enables a subconscious desire for something fun or new.

This phenomenon disrupts organized project execution (*Balls in a tube*). It also negatively impacts project execution velocity in the N-1 matrix space.

What are the types of distractions? Contributors needing a mental health diversion. Other project managers showing up with that new cool thing to work on. Managers asking for that "one easy quick thing."

Should you encounter this phenomenon, keep in mind that explicitly calling out a contributor's loss of focus is bad form. Contributors demonstrating this behavior will not appreciate the public shaming. Often, they do not even realize the behavior is happening.

There is a synergy to be found between the *Shiny-object distraction* and *Distraction elimination* concepts. Aggressively delivering *Distraction elimination* dramatically reduces the potential for a *Shiny-object distraction*.

Hey, I am working here

Most employers are only interested in employing people when there is work to do. People without work to do will be promoted to customer status. That is to say they will no longer be employed.

In the corporate environment, this fact often drives "looking busy" behavior bordering on mania. A full meeting schedule, one hundred emails a day, etc. People working ten to twelve hours a day. So much to do.

Delivered value becomes secondary to demonstrable work effort. Digging holes and filling them, so to speak.

The phenomenon observed here: contributors making work more complex and with a higher-than-necessary work content. They stretch expended efforts, processes, and tasks to appear as overloaded as possible.

There is an element of risk avoidance being demonstrated here. Most likely this is a corporate environment with strict adherence to N-1. The slightest hint of slack in the labor supply and someone is going to be released to pursue other opportunities.

Knowing about these risk-avoidance situations and engaging with sensitivity is key. If this is the situation, it is important to not publicly acknowledge it. Instead, try a modified *Distraction elimination*. Present project tasks without the "filler." Accelerate project execution without upsetting the busy work system perceived as necessary for people to keep their jobs.

This book is about practical project management solutions. Not solving the world's problems. This kind of survival mechanism will be baked into the company culture. Tilting at this windmill will just bring you trouble.

A wise project manager can leverage this well of untapped productivity.

Speed is not an N-1/matrix feature

The N-1/matrix project management environment has many useful features.

Speed is not one of them.

The N-1 work overload, lack of genuine authority when requesting attention from contributors, and the relative autonomy matrixed contributors enjoy in prioritizing tasks slows down project execution.

This is not about efficiency or per unit cost of effort. Assuming the *Angels on a pinhead* approach is being avoided, N-1/matrix delivers on the promise of maximum output from a minimum of resources.

The challenge is in planning and maintaining sequential execution of tasks. Keeping contributors focused and on time is the observed phenomenon.

Frustration at the slow progress of project execution is a common project manager problem. The compartmentalized nature of contributors and the relative autonomy they enjoy require strategies (*In person for maximum effect, Be positive, Constructive persistence, Balls in a tube, The 98% problem, A little speculative paranoia goes a long way, Distraction elimination, The easy button, Building bridges*). N-1/matrix environments are awash in people-centric phenomena. Leveraging these opportunities through skill development is the foundation of this book.

If you have observed it always seems to take longer to deliver than expected, you are not wrong. Maximizing project velocity in the N-1/matrix space is an expert-level achievement.

So, it's not just me?

This chapter shares the phenomena observed with N-1 and the matrix from a project management standpoint. Not only are the individual phenomena associated with each concept, but there are additional dynamics generated by the two interacting with each other.

The matrix applied on a global scale introduces other considerations. Building up the skills that address the project management phenomena by acknowledging cultural nuance.

Acknowledging these phenomena opens a path to developing the tools needed to address the modern corporate N-1 and matrix environment impact on project management. Deployment of an array of skills addressing project management challenges delivers synergistic benefits in the combined N-1 / matrix space.

Did We Learn Anything?

The potential for unlimited growth at zero cost.

Developing the people-centric skills addressing the phenomena presented in this book has no significant cost. Productivity improves, expense decreases. With no capital expenditure. The in-between space in every project is waiting to be addressed.

It's like magic.

Not really. Skill development is a long-term commitment involving a lot of hard work.

Acknowledgement of the phenomena and skill development will improve your abilities in navigating the human equation and executing larger/longer and more complex efforts. With experience, you will begin anticipating challenges that in the past would have brought your project management efforts to a standstill.

Success breeds success. A demonstrated track record of delivering projects and meeting expectations can make future projects easier. Build those skills, hone your craft, and as you improve, contributors will accept collaboration more readily. Your success is their success. This mutual synergy becomes a win-win for everyone. Efficiency and quality improve. Sunshine and unicorns, etc. You get the picture.

Truly developing your craft will take thousands of hours of hard work, learning from others, making mistakes, and applying yourself. Each project, each attempt at developing a skill, will deliver incremental improvements. There will also be leaps forward in understanding and effectiveness to look forward to.

One of the goals of this book is to provide visibility. Provoking thought and inspiring action.

If you are going to play, play to win. In project management, the project managers and their skills – especially in the people space – are key to success.